Foot

CW01636810

DISCOVERING GOD

Over the next 100 days you are invited to explore the Bible and discover some of the richness of God's character. This will give you a taste of what friendship with God involves. *Discovering God* is the second book in the *Foothold* series.

Although *Foothold* is ideal for use with the *Contemporary English Version* (CEV), it can be easily used with other modern versions of the Bible. In this copy of *Foothold* the CEV text has been quoted and in specific instances, The *New International Version* (NIV), *Good News Bible* (GNB), *Living Bible, Jerusalem Bible*, and Eugene Peterson's *The Message*, Navpress, Colorado, 1993.

Set time aside and establish a simple pattern for using this book.

Happy travelling!

Scripture Union
Resources for Ministry Unit
PO Box 77, Lidcombe, NSW 2141, Australia

Prepared by Harry Cotter based on material by Derek Williams
Editor: Rena Pritchard
Design and Layout: Allan Weatherall. Insight Graphics, Melbourne
Cover Photo: Terry Boyd
Printed by Jenkin Buxton Printers Pty Ltd, Box Hill
ISBN 0-949720-55-0

Foothold

HOW TO USE FOOTHOLD

Most of us find it hard work to create the space and make the time to be alone and quiet, even for a few minutes each day. The struggle is worth it, especially when we use these hard-won minutes of solitude to focus on God, to make room for him in our lives.

WHAT TIME OF DAY?

The tradition of the time-tested discipline of the early morning 'Quiet Time' is one many Christians find helpful. The godly missionary pioneer Hudson Taylor used to say 'Do not have your concert first and then tune your instrument afterwards. Begin the day with the word of God and get first of all into harmony with Him.' For myself, I find this pattern the best, though it took me many years to establish. But it is only a tradition, not a law, and for some people it is just not workable. Don't give up: early morning, lunch-break, bedtime, Sunday evening… Find what works for you and make a regular appointment with God a high priority. It may be even better spent if it is shared with another who also wants to come to grips with God and what God says to us.

HOW TO GO ABOUT IT?

Try to keep a balance between *head* and *heart*, between studying the Bible and seeking God's presence, for both are serious matters. Instead of rushing in, we need to ***prepare*** ourselves for what might follow (See the article on 'Meeting with God', on page 9).

Read the passage carefully, more than once.
A different translation can help.

Explore what God has to say to you in the passage.

THESE QUESTIONS MIGHT HELP YOU.

1. What does the passage say to me? Is there a promise, a command, an example, a warning?
2. What do I discover about God?
3. What do I learn about people and their relationship with God or each other?

PREPARE

READ

EXPLORE

RESPOND

Compare your thoughts with the comments in *Foothold*. These comments are not designed to explain every problem but to encourage you to develop one or two lines of thought. To help you remember what you have read, mark verses in your Bible with a line in the margin or a highlighter. Many people find that keeping a notebook or journal is valuable. If you have unanswered questions about the reading, find a Christian friend or a helpful book such as a Bible commentary. Consider forming a group where you can discuss questions like those above (see 'Using *Foothold* in a Group', page 45).

Think how God might want you to **respond** to what you have read (see 'Responding to God's Word', page 65).

Part of your response will be to **pray**: sometimes prayer will just flow from the reading, sometimes it may help to have a simple format of your own. My favourite one goes:

P - S - A - L - M

PRAISE	the God you've read about
SURRENDER	to him in repentance & worship
ASK	for the help you need to live for him
LOVE	bring the names of your family, friends and enemies before God. A list of people and organisations, distributed over the days of the week, can assist you.
MEDITATE	find a thought to take into the day. Keep note of your prayers as a reminder to you to expect answers to them.

DAY 1: GO ON, LORD - I'M LISTENING!

Our God, the Creator of the universe, is huge, powerful and glorious, more beautiful than sunrise, more dangerous than lightning, far beyond the reach of our tiny minds. God can seem very distant when we think about him in this way, But the wonderful truth to hold tightly together with his greatness is that this awesome God of ours *has* spoken to human beings — and *still* speaks.

As you read your Bible over the next few days, pray that you will learn, as Samuel did, to listen better to what God says.

1 Samuel chapter 3

The old priest Eli had allowed standards to slip badly at the sacred place, so very few people were listening to God (1). Was God far away and communicating less or was no-one listening?

This incident shows how God chose Samuel, first of a new line of prophets who would speak out for him clearly and strongly. Later, because of Samuel's response, God could speak through him using his background, training and personality. Samuel and the other prophets, said Peter, were 'carried along by the Holy Spirit', like a ship driven by the wind (2 Peter 1:21, NIV).

God could have shown himself to Samuel in visions, or miracles. Why do you think he chose to use words?

Samuel might have developed a swollen head as a result of the way God had chosen him, and Eli's pride might also have been severely dented. Then it would have been harder for both to hear clearly what God wanted to tell them. How *did* they respond? (8-10,18) Perhaps God is trying to penetrate your thoughts to direct you to something new? Pray that you will recognise his voice, then have the humility to respond.

DAY 2: GOD SPEAKS THROUGH CREATION

'I often think of the heavens your hands have made, and of the moon and stars you put in place. Then I ask, "Why do you care about us humans? Why are you concerned for us weaklings?"'

(Psalm 8:3-4)

Think about this for a while. Ask God the same question.

Psalm 19:1-6

The psalm writer was overwhelmed with God's creation. He wondered why God would bother to care about him. If we look hard at 'the heavens' — and the earth's living things, scientific laws, etc. — what do they tell us about God? On the evidence of creation, how sure can you be that God the Creator exists? Put an X where you fit on the scale below. Don't worry where you come on the scale.

100% sure 50% sure 0% sure

We all have doubts like the psalm writer. If God *is* there, what can we discover about him from his creation? For example, from the laws of physics it's an odds-on bet that God would have to be a great mathematician! But what else? Tick any of the things below that you know to be true of God from your observation of the created universe.

❑ Loving ❑ Wise ❑ Personal ❑ Good ❑ Powerful
❑ Orderly ❑ Holy ❑ Other

God, you seem so immense — how can I possibly worship you? Be patient with me as I bring my doubts to you. Help me to resolve them one by one. You are the greatest artist of all. Your works are more exquisite than the best artwork, sculpture or music on earth. You show us your power and your wonderful sense of design.

DAY 3: GOD SPEAKS THROUGH THE BIBLE

Thankyou, God, that you want to be in touch with me, that you already meet me more than half way. I want to reach out to you, too.

Psalm 19:7-14

In the previous reading we saw that while the creation is a powerful witness to God's existence and greatness, it is a limited witness. If God were just a remote Great Mathematician in the Sky, it would be hard to trust him, or to believe he had any personal interest in us.

But our God wants us to know him better than this, and has given us more than creation to go on — we have been given his written word. What qualities of God's word does the writer, King David value? (7-10)

On a human level, speech often reflects character ('Your words show what is in your hearts', Luke 6:45). If God's word is perfect, what does this tell us about God himself?

At the time this psalm was written, the Scriptures consisted mostly of 'The Law', the first five books of our Old Testament. Today, we can apply what David said to the much fuller word of God that we have in the Old and New Testaments.

David got tremendous help from his Bible reading: moral and spiritual strength to obey God (7), wisdom to make good decisions (7), the peace and joy of a clear conscience (8,11-13). What else can you find?

We hope that with the help of *Foothold* your Bible reading will be a source of practical help and inspiration. However, to be honest, it can lose its excitement from time to time. What will you do if or when this happens? Talk to a more experienced Christian friend? Pray about it? Give up?

DAY 4: GOD SPEAKS THROUGH JESUS

'Open my mind and let me discover the wonders of your Law.' (Psalm 119:18) The writer seems to be saying to God: 'There are wonderful things in your law; I want to understand them, but by myself, I don't have the ability. So I need your help, Lord — please.'

Hebrews 1:1-4

Many early Christians were strangers to the Jewish faith, but this remarkable letter was written to former Jews. Because of the threat of severe persecution, it seems some of them were wondering whether to 'hang in' with Christ, or go back to being Jews.

The author (whose name we don't know) writes to support them. He encourages them to persevere by writing about God's astonishing Son, Jesus Christ, and what he has done for them.

Jesus is God's Voice. God spoke wonderfully but incompletely in the Old Testament. Now he reveals himself fully and finally in his Son. How do we know what God is like? We look at Jesus; he 'is the exact likeness of God's own being'! (3, GNB)

Jesus is God's Son. Jesus is God's authentic voice and image because he is God's Son; he has acted on God's behalf in creating the universe and holding it together. Surely the hands that did that are strong enough to hold us, no matter how great the pressures!

Peter, James and John were told by God to 'Listen to what he says!' after seeing Jesus completely changed on the mountain (Mark 9:7). They were dazzled by his glory. Read Hebrews 2:1. How can we avoid drifting away? What captures your imagination in today's reading?

DAY 5: ALL THE ANGELS WORSHIP HIM

Angels bow down before you, worship and adore,
for you have the words of eternal life,
you are Jesus Christ the Lord. (M. Ford)

Hebrews 1:5-14

From fairies to UFO's, extra-terrestrial creatures have always hovered on the edges of human imagination. Maybe they *do* exist! The Bible says that angels were created by God. We know that from time to time people encounter them today. The community to whom this letter was written would certainly have believed angels existed. They must have wondered if Jesus was one — the greatest one of course. 'No way!', says our writer. In the conflicts of the unseen spiritual world God's angels are there, helping God's people (14); but they are only helpers and messengers.

Jesus alone is God's Son (5), *Jesus alone* reigns for eternity with God the Father over the whole creation, and *Jesus alone* is to be worshipped — by people *and* angels.

Are you in a situation where you feel powerless? Do you need special help? Or, does someone you know need help? Ask Jesus directly for assistance. He may send a 'messenger' (angel or human) to strengthen and encourage you or your friend. Help may come in unexpected ways. Remember, Jesus is not too remote to understand your situation. One of the benefits of his having lived an ordinary life on earth was that he experienced many of the situations we face. Try sharing your problem with him.

A good habit to get into is to write down your prayer requests. Review them regularly and note how and when they are answered. You may be surprised by what you learn. And, remember to thank God when your prayers are answered.

MEETING WITH GOD

Getting to know God is like talking on the telephone to someone you have not met. As you discover common interests you begin to share things with each other. Like all true friendships, friendship with God cannot be rushed. Approaching it like a 'work assignment' won't guarantee a worthwhile encounter. Be intentional in your awareness of God and open to new directions.

A variety of people have found the following suggestions helpful:

Pray this Psalm, 'Open my mind and let me discover the wonders of your Law'. (Psalm 119:18)

Be silent and focus on God. Don't worry that you don't yet know much about God or his character.

Let some of the Bible's ***symbols*** like water, seeds, bread, a candle or picture be a focus for exploring an aspect of God's truth.

Reflect on your everyday life, thoughts, things done, things left undone. If some barrier prevents you discussing a matter with God, admit this and ask for and accept his forgiveness. Nothing is too bad or ordinary to bring before God.

Listen to meditative music to still the mind and prepare for listening.

Focus on one aspect of God's nature or a phrase from your Bible reading until it fills your senses.

If the words of a chorus, hymn or popular tune speak to you, ***say, hum, or sing*** them as a prayer.

Stretch out your hands, palms down and close them. Imagine that in them are things that come between you and God: idols, worries, excuses, pride. Let them go. Now turn your open, empty hands upward to receive whatever God wants to give you: unexpected gifts and blessings, special responsibilities.

Tune your mind to God by using the 'Prepare' section of your reading.

Check point A

GOD THE CREATOR

INTRODUCTION TO READINGS 6 TO 14, IN PSALMS, GENESIS, EXODUS AND ISAIAH.

We began *Foothold* with readings to encourage us to listen to God in a variety of ways. Now, we move into our main theme, to learn what God is like. We look first at some Old Testament passages which tell us about God's work in creation.

The first passage is from Psalms. The Psalms are songs. They were used by the people of God in ancient times to express their deepest feelings about God and their own experiences.

We then move to Genesis, the first book of the Bible, for its account of creation. This wonderful prose-poem focuses on the essential truths that God wants us to know.

Following that, in three readings from the Exodus story, we see some principles that God lays down for his people's creativity in every generation.

Finally, the prophet Isaiah describes God the Creator, comparing him with the gods invented by people. These readings are also in poetic form, full of picture language. The secret of reading such passages is to let the picture spin around in your imagination. Look for the truth behind the image. Don't worry if everything isn't crystal clear. The Australian poet, Les Murray says, 'Poems are no good if you understand everything in them.'!

Some of these passages were written 2500 years or so ago. Others have been passed down orally through countless generations. Yet, brought together, they are like the panes of a great stained-glass window, providing a vivid composite picture of our majestic Creator God.

DAY 6: MY GOD, YOU ARE VERY GREAT

The prayer preceding all prayers is
'May it be the real I who speaks.
May it be the real Thou that I speak to'. (*C.S. Lewis*)

Lord, help me to know more about who you are, so that when I pray, I can talk to you freely like today's psalm writer.

Psalm 104

As our writer looks at his world, he becomes excited about it — and about the God who made it.

God is greater than the world (1-4): God is not part of the world, as some religions teach, but greater than it, delighting in it. 'He's got the whole world in his hand.' **God designed the world** (5-9): The astronomer Sir James Jeans once said: 'The universe begins to look more like a great thought than a great machine.' **God provides good things for his creatures.** Do you give thanks to God for all he provides, such as giving thanks before meals? Do you sometimes misuse and spoil his creation or greedily take more than your share of it? **God's work is wonderfully varied** (24-26) Variety in creation shouts out that our God is a creator with an extravagant enthusiasm and generosity —and a great sense of humour.

And as for the duck, I think God must have smiled a bit
Seeing those bright eyes blink on the day He fashioned it.
And He's probably laughing still at the sound that came out of its bill.

F.W. Harvey, 'Ducks'.

The 19th century poet, Dante G. Rossetti wrote, 'The worst moment for the atheist is when he is really thankful and has nobody to thank.' List the things you wish to thank God for today and express your thanks.

DAY 7: CHARGED WITH THE GRANDEUR OF GOD

'Praised be my Lord God for all his creatures, especially for our brother the sun, who brings us the day and who brings us the light; fair is he and shines with a very great splendour; O Lord, he signifies you to us!' *(St Francis of Assisi)*

Genesis 1:1-19

Scientists write books about 'The First Three Minutes' after the big bang. Christians debate whether creation happened in six 24-hour days. The writer of Genesis is talking about the big questions, the ones science cannot begin to answer. He would not have been interested in these theories. His timeless description, more a painting or poem than a textbook or printout, tells us that at the beginning and heart of the universe, lies

- not a snakepit of quarrelling gods (as other early creation stories describe)
- not a chaos where only chance is in control
- not a vague impersonal force

but a personal God, who, of his own choice, creates to fulfil his own purposes.

- He is a God of indescribable power, who only had to speak, and it *was*.
- He is a God of order, who created a world of order, one in which we can expect to find the regularities which scientists look for.

If you know this song, why not sing it (aloud, or silently, according to where you are!)?

O Lord my God, when I in awesome wonder
consider all the works Thy hand hath made,
I see the stars, I hear the mighty thunder,
Thy power throughout the universe displayed,
Then sings my soul, my Saviour God, to Thee,
how great Thou art, how great Thou art! *(Stuart Kittine)*

DAY 8: THE IDENTITY GOD GAVE US

'You have made us for yourself, O Lord, and our hearts are restless until they find their rest in you.' *(St Augustine)*. When *your* heart is restless, where do you look for rest? Where does your heart find solid ground?

Genesis 1:20-31

What are we? Is the writer saying that because we were made on the same day as them, we are just animals? Animals, yes, but not *just* animals: they were made (25), we were *created*. In the original Hebrew of the Bible, the word *bara* (27) is a different word, describing 'something-out-of-nothing', a 'something-totally-new' creation (used also in 1,21).

When asking, 'What am I?', I am compelled to ask other searching questions such as:

If I am in some significant way *like* God (for example, can make moral choices, can know and worship God?), what does this say about how I see myself?

If both men and women are created *equally* in the image of God, what does this imply about the way we treat each other?

If the people I live with, work with or have some influence over also bear the imprint of God, what does this tell me about how I may, or may not treat them?

If part of our original job-description (26,28) was to be God's 'middle management' over his other creatures, what does this say about how we should treat his creation?

It's a bit overwhelming living with the knowledge that I'm made in your image. But, ***Thankyou***, God, for making me who I am. ***Sorry***, God, for the way I have sometimes treated others you have made (especially… and…). ***Please***, God, renew your image in me.

DAY 9: TIME TO WORK, TIME TO REST

God, with a universe to care for, has a space for you. Make space for him: push back the intruding worries and pleasures, give this time wholly to him, make it a mini-Sabbath.

Exodus 31:12-18

It isn't clear here what it means for God to rest (17) since he doesn't get tired. It seems to say that this rhythm of work and rest is built into creation, much as a car's regular servicing schedule is 'built into' its design and manufacture. If we think that we, through cleverness or strength, can run our lives better by disregarding the Maker's instructions, then we are in serious trouble.

Too many, in hot pursuit of worthwhile (or worthless) goals, are stretched to the limit, taking families and colleagues with them (see Exodus 23:12). Others are also off balance because they give *less* than full value to the days allowed for work.

This principle of one week's work, one day's rest, is valid for all. For God's people, there is a second principle. To recharge a battery, you need first to take the load off, then to connect it to the main power source. The Sabbath was a day of *holy* rest, given to God (15). From the earliest days Christians have come together on Sundays to praise God, hear his word and encourage one another. Our way of life is to be a sign (12) to God, to ourselves, and to others, that we are his people, different.

Think over:

❍ How smoothly is my work/rest rhythm running?

❍ Is God at the focus of my leisure time?

Pray today for people whose life doesn't easily fit with these ideas — shift workers, church workers, parents with small children …

DAY 10: CHILDREN OF A GIVING GOD

Thou hast given so much to me,
Give one thing more — a grateful heart. (George Herbert)

Exodus 35:20-29

Imagine yourself one of the Israelites, camped in the eerie echoing granite valley below Mount Sinai. Moses, your leader has been up on the mountain for nearly six weeks (read about it in chapters 24 and 32). Now he comes down, face shining with the reflected glory of God — it's been quite a week.

Moses announces to his people that God wants them to build a place where they can meet with him to worship and make sacrifices to him. The project will include a tabernacle (a tent), two altars, an ark (a wooden box a metre or so long to hold and transport the flat stones with the Ten Commandments written on them), a curtained courtyard for over 1000 people, gold plates, robes for the priests and so on (see chapters 25-30 for the details). Moses says, God wants his people, including you, to donate the materials to make all these items.

But you have very few possessions: a few gold rings and precious stones kept to provide for your daughter's dowry, some wool you were saving to make a new blanket for winter, some olive oil... Does Moses really need them for this strange construction? What will happen to your daughter?

God's people were moved, not just to warm feelings, but to measurable, costly action. Some gave possessions, some gave skills and service.

God could have provided miraculously for everything required, but he chose to give his people the privilege of sharing in the project.

Is God offering you a similar opportunity?

DAY 11: UNWRAP YOUR GIFTS

I am only a spark - Make me a fire.
I am only a string - Make me a lyre.
I am only a drop - Make me a fountain.
I am only an ant hill - Make me a mountain.
I am only a feather - Make me a wing.
I am only a rag - Make me a king! *(a prayer from Mexico)*

Exodus 35:30-36:7

One of our daughters asked me to make a sand-pit for her toddler. A simple design came to mind. Using old hardwood fence palings, our grandson soon had a new sand-pit, and I had a warm feeling of satisfaction!

God has made us like himself in our ability to 'create' things, and to enjoy doing so. Our gift may bring into being a garden, a dinner or a speech. Whatever it is, it is unique and it is God's gift to us.

In today's text, notice how this particular example of creativity came about:

- God's Spirit was given (31) to make Bezalel's 'natural' talent effective in God's service.
- those with gifts shared them with others (34).
- the whole jigsaw was quietly pulled together.

Read 4-7 again.

What creative thing could you do that might become a 'lightning conductor' for God's Spirit to work in ways like this in your church or group?

Discover your gifts — ask God to show you what they are, ask other Christians, try them out. ***Dedicate*** your gifts to God — thank God for them, enjoy them, use them for the good of others (but do not flaunt them in a proud manner). ***Develop*** your gifts, as God gives you energy and direction.

DAY 12: GOD KNOWS WHAT HE IS DOING

Pray this aloud (or sing it!)

Change my heart, O God, make it ever true;
change my heart, O God, may I be like you.
You are the potter, I am the clay;
mould me and make me, this is what I pray... *(Eddie Espinosa)*

Isaiah 45:5-11

The story is told of the funeral where a church elder was a little too honest. He gave thanks for the life of the dear brother who had been used so abundantly by God 'to try the patience of all of us'! It is true that even people who do not honour God, nevertheless can find themselves serving him (5).

This was the situation the people of Israel were about to face in exile in Babylon (see the next reading for the details of who and why).

To help them understand what he was about to do, God gave the people of Israel this message through Isaiah. He warned them that they would not understand what he was going to do, that they would strongly question his motives in putting them into such a strange situation (9-11), but they were not to lose confidence in him.

Do you ever find yourself questioning God;
complaining to him?
For example,

❍ Why did you let my dad (friend/baby etc.) die?
❍ Why are we always short of money, when others — who don't work so hard — have plenty?
❍ Why did you make my nose/legs/hair... like they are?

God doesn't seem to mind us asking questions like this (the Psalms, like Psalm 73, are full of them), but based on this passage, how do you think he would answer you?

DAY 13: GOD'S IN CONTROL

'Only to our intellect is he incomprehensible — not to our love.' *The Cloud of Unknowing (14th C.)*

Isaiah 45:12-17

Cyrus the Great, King of Persia is the Cyrus of verse 13 (and 1,2,5). Within 20 years of coming to the throne, this amazing man led his army to victory over every kingdom in the Middle East, including finally, mighty Babylon. Isaiah tells us it was God who gave him his victories (1) but in a clay tablet written at the time, Cyrus attributed his success to the god Marduk (5). Having conquered, he surprised everyone by declaring that the captured peoples deported to Babylon were now free to return home (13). So the victory was for Cyrus, but the salvation was for Israel (17).

We don't know exactly when Isaiah wrote this chapter, but the Jewish historian Josephus records that Cyrus was shown a copy of the prophecy when he entered Babylon. God prepared his people to trust he was in control, even though the person he was to use did not know him.

Early in the 1960s, the writer Helmut Thielicke wrote: 'When the drama of history is over... all the great figures of history — Pharaoh, Alexander the Great, Charlemagne, Churchill, Stalin, Mao Tse Tung — will realise they have been bit actors in a drama produced by Another.'

World events puzzle us. They worry us just as much as the personal anxieties and crises we thought about in the last reading. It hard for us to see God in these events, because we are limited by time and space. But Isaiah tells us to trust that God will work out his purposes. Next time you watch or hear or read the daily news, be encouraged by this.

DAY 14: THERE IS NO OTHER!

Lord, help me to see what you want me to see, that I may be what you want me to be.

Isaiah 45:18-25

Imagine you are a Jew in Babylon. Your people have been there for nearly 70 years. You are confronted daily by the arrogant success of people who worship other gods. How do you feel about *your* God?

Crushed by a lifetime of exile and defeat, the people of Israel are finding it hard to hear Isaiah's message. But he tells them again about this God who is about to set them free. Isaiah's poetry ranges from the distant past to a future that even we, in our time, have yet to experience.

Isaiah tells them that, though God is hidden (15), he is not dead. He is revealed in the majesty of creation (18), and by the truth of the words he speaks (19).

He tells them that, contrary to appearances, it is the other gods who are the powerless nonentities; there simply *is* no other god (21). Read verses 13-19 of chapter 44 for a scurrilous description of idolatry. Would this book have passed the Imperial Babylonian Censors?

Then comes the bombshell: God is not only Israel's God — he is to become everyone's God (22). One day, whether people like it or not, everyone would know this (23).

After years of seeing the success of those who deliberately ignore God or defiantly worship other things or systems, Christians can feel discouraged. But Isaiah's words come through for us, fresh and shining, in the promise that 'at the name of Jesus everyone will bow down ... everyone will openly agree, "Jesus Christ is Lord!"' (Philippians 2:10-11)

THIS BOOK SPEAKS WITH AUTHORITY

'Hasn't Science disproved the Bible?'

'It's definitely inspired, just like Shakespeare.'

'Parts of it are great, but we've moved on a bit, haven't we?'

Ideas like these are common. Why do Christians continue to claim that the Bible has such powerful authority in their faith and life? All the historic churches, Catholic, Orthodox, Lutheran, Reformed, Anglican, Pentecostal etc. are founded on this basis, in some cases placing the Bible's authority alongside their traditions.

The biblical writers frequently claim God's inspiration and authority for themselves and for each other. The prophets often say 'This is what the Lord says…', and both Paul and Peter in the New Testament claim that Old Testament writers were led by the Holy Spirit (2 Timothy 3:16; 2 Peter 1:21).

Countless believers have found that the Bible hangs together, makes sense, and generally 'works' for them. It has a 'ring of truth' that no other book has.

But the main reason we accept the authority of Scripture is because Jesus did. He constantly said things like 'It is written…' or 'the Son of Man (meaning himself) goes as it is written of him…'. Whether the consequences were pleasant or not, Jesus felt compelled to obey what was written there.

SOME THINGS NEED TO BE MADE CLEAR:

The Bible was written by human writers. God did not over-ride their personalities. However, we can believe that he involved himself in their circumstances, so that while the words were their own, at the same time they were the words of God.

Errors have occurred as manuscripts were copied, or in translation from the original languages — Hebrew and Greek. By comparing different copies, some errors have been found, but they are few and insignificant. Present-day translations are very reliable.

God's revelation was progressive, so some earlier teaching (such as the Old Testament laws relating to sacrifices) has been superseded by the new and better way we have in Jesus.

Words should be read in context. For example, the Bible does say, more than once, that there is no God. However, looking at Psalm 14, we can see it is the fool who says this!

Bible scholars help to solve problems of the kind described above. Their task is to give us as accurate a text as possible. Sometimes there is doubt on the authenticity of particular words or passages which may derive from a later tradition. Thus, some passages are labelled 'possibly genuine', or 'a later addition'.

A few scholars deny the Bible is inspired, finding God hardly relevant. The media pick up on their more outrageous ideas. But most scholars dearly love God's word and bring fresh insights to Christians. They struggle with and discuss the academic problems encountered. God still speaks to us through the text which has been faithfully handed down to us to read. We must use our God-given minds, and ask questions so we may understand what it is saying to us. There are solid grounds for accepting the Bible is substantially as God intended it to be. If God is there, standing behind the word he has spoken, then we must accept its authority.

Checkpoint B

GOD'S NATURE IN JESUS

INTRODUCTION TO READINGS 15 TO 20 IN JOHN'S GOSPEL AND PAUL'S LETTER TO THE COLOSSIANS.

Sometimes things don't go, after all,
from bad to worse...
Sometimes our best efforts do not go
amiss; sometimes we do as we meant to.
The sun will sometimes melt a field of sorrow
that seemed hard frozen: may it happen for you. (Sheenagh Pugh)

This gem seems to say that while 'Murphy's Law' ('If something can go wrong, it will go wrong.') is our common experience, it should not be so. Our human dilemma is that we sense a huge gulf between ourselves and God, the creator of the universe. We feel completely alone. Not only our human relationships are affected by this gulf, but the whole of creation seems doomed. Nothing we do seems to have any effect on making things better. We are surrounded by pain and decay (Romans 8:18-22), alienated from God (Colossians 1:21) and each other.

These readings help us to explore what God in his goodness has done about our problem. In a nutshell, God sent us his Son, Jesus. This was too great a mental leap for most of Jesus' contemporaries. In John we see them trying to work out who this remarkable person is — but refusing to accept the truth of the evidence.

Some thirty years after Jesus' death, a newly established church at Colossae suffers from a rash of false teachers making wild speculations. To give these Christians an anchor, Paul begins his letter with a dazzling picture of the 'Cosmic Christ'.

Once we grasp that Jesus *is* God in the flesh, we can turn this idea inside out. To know what God is like, we can now look at Jesus (John 1:18).

DAY 15: CONTENT WITH SECOND BEST?

When we come to the end of our hoarded resources,
Our Father's full giving has only begun.
(Annie Johnson Flint)

John 5:1-15

Jesus asks, 'Do you *want* to be healed?', but the man doesn't hear the question. After 38 years of waiting, despair is a familiar comfort, like an old pair of jeans. It's easier to give the routine explanation, 'my problem is…', than think about starting life again.

Critics said that since this pool with five porches had not been found, the pool and therefore probably the whole story, was probably invented by John. But excavations in Jerusalem have now revealed just such a pool, in exactly the place described. The Jewish religious leaders were, as ever, alert to the nit-picking details of the law and blind to God's great purposes of salvation (9,10). In this story, Jesus warns the man that his sickness is in some way linked with his sin (14). This kind of cause and effect is recognised by doctors today as a real possibility. But the New Testament does not normally make this connection (see John 9:1-3) and we should not jump to this conclusion for ourselves or anyone else.

Is there an area of your life which obstructs the possibility of change? Why not open it up to the living Jesus who has the power to enable you to change. It may help to ask a Christian minister or close friend to pray with you about it.

Does your church retain traditions that keep people, especially those on the fringe, from following Christ? Where is the best place to question the purposes of these traditions so that change is able to occur? What can you contribute?

DAY 16: WHAT IS JESUS TO YOU?

Think through what Jesus means to you. If Jesus were not there with you, in you, what would be missing in your life? Write it down. Thank him.

John 5:16-29

Who is Jesus? We see here how conflict with Jewish leaders led Jesus to talk about himself and the Father. Some remarkable claims emerge. He claims to be 'the Son of God' (25). In a general sense, all people are God's children, by creation. More specifically, we become children of God only when we receive Jesus and are born (again) — see John 1:12-13. But Jesus talks about 'My Father' (17). What he describes (19-23) is a wonderful 'one-heart, one-mind' identification of obedience and love with his father. No wonder the Jews complain that he is 'making himself equal with God' (18).

We need to weigh these claims: the next reading looks at some of the evidence to back them up. For now we must accept that they offer us three logical conclusions:

❍ Jesus was BAD — a cheat, a con-man

❍ Jesus was MAD — self-deluded, a megalomaniac

❍ Jesus was GOD — he was what he said

The one thing we cannot say is 'He was just a good man'. No 'good man' would make claims like these.

Are you sure of your conclusion? If Jesus was God, then his claims to be the giver of life (21), and the judge of all people (22,27,30) must be taken seriously. But what is he *to you*? Giver of life, Saviour, Lord and Friend? Or the One whose perfect justice will be forced to leave you standing hopeless and helpless on that final day? Take the time to check out and test Jesus' claims.

DAY 17: YOU CAN LEAD A HORSE TO WATER . . .

'Blessed Lord, you have caused all holy scriptures to be written for our learning: grant us... to hear them, read, mark, learn, and inwardly digest them.' (*Anglican Book of Common Prayer*)

John 5:30-47

Jesus has made some heavy claims.
Here he shows he has supporting evidence.
John the Baptist (31-35). The Jews respected his witness (see John 1:19-31) but John simply pointed towards Jesus.
Jesus' own actions (36). Miracles are too easily imitated to be the *only* proof of a person's genuineness, but Jesus' works were always good, reflecting God's nature.
The Father (37,38).
The Scriptures (39-40, 45-47). The Jewish Scriptures, our Old Testament, contain hundreds of prophecies fulfilled by Jesus. Many Jewish contemporaries of Jesus read the Scriptures with closed minds, looking to them to buttress their preconceived ideas. Unwilling to surrender their position of religious power and privilege, these Jews were blind to the evidence of Jesus' true nature. They lost out, making him very sad (Luke 19:41-44).

This can also apply to us. Despite the Bible being inexpensive and easy to get, its treasures remain closed to proud, blind, stubborn, prejudiced people.

Try to keep your mind open to new insights. Here are some suggestions for making your Bible reading more productive:
Read: try reading aloud, using two different translations
Mark: zoom in on core ideas; pick them out with a pencil line in the margin, or use colours
Learn: pick out a phrase or verse and memorise it
Digest: 'chew the cud of the Word' (a nice phrase, from the 2nd C *Epistle of Barnabas*). Turn over in your mind the implications for yourself of what you have read.

DAY 18: CHRIST UNFATHOMABLE, UNFASHIONABLE

'We look at this Son and see the God who cannot be seen. We look at this Son and see God's original purpose in everything created.' Lord, help me to see Jesus today, and in him to see you, and in him to see myself as you would have me be.

Colossians 1:15-20

This passage would be edited out of a 'politically correct' New Testament. In an age where we pretend that one religion is as good as another, many cannot accept 'intolerant' claims like this. But God's truth has a way of surviving the fashions.

Christ the Son: Did Christ come into being only when he was born in Bethlehem? (15-17)

Christ Supreme: Was Jesus just a superman, a very great teacher, the best man ever? (18,19)

Christ Sufficient: Do we need another spiritual being or power, apart from Christ, to do it for us (20) so we can be reconciled with God and brought back into friendship with him?

No! No!! No!!!

Do you want Christ, the eternal creator Son, to be active in your life — building, strengthening, re-creating? How active? Are you prepared for changes in direction, emphasis, habits?

How supreme is Christ in your church? In your worship, your programs, your evangelism… ? Does something need to change?

Is Christ holding things together for you (17), or are you worried and confused? It has been said, 'If all our doings are "begun, continued, and ended" in him, then all things *will* hold together for us.' This will be wonderfully and *fully* true in heaven, and is wonderfully and *partly* true on earth. Share your worries with Christ and start sampling and enjoying the real thing!

DAY 19: ONCE YOU WERE . . . BUT NOW

Slowly repeat *The Jesus Prayer*: 'Lord Jesus Christ, Son of God, have mercy on me' several times. Each time emphasise a different word. *(The prayer is from the Orthodox tradition.)*

Colossians 1:21-23

Life is full of 'watershed' experiences: leaving school, getting married... We can compare what life was like before and after the event.

Becoming a Christian is also a turning point. It may be sudden, like the change from unemployment to employment (or, more sadly, vice versa). Or, it may be gradual, like the change occurring in a slimmer on a diet. Either way, it should be the most profound change in our entire life (13).

Before, we were at odds with the ruler of the universe (21), not just ignorant or apathetic, but with our backs turned on him, putting ourselves first in our thinking and in our doing.

When there is a breakdown in relationships, people remain at loggerheads — until one person takes the first step. This is what God has done in the death of Christ (22). He offers us peace, reconciliation. If we accept it, the past is forgotten; we're accepted as if we were faultless and innocent (22). But this 'after' state of affairs, like any relationship, needs to be worked at (23).

In a hair-restorer advertisement, the printer managed to place the 'before' and 'after' photos the wrong way round! Sometimes when people become Christians we almost prefer them as they were before — like the little girl who prayed 'Lord, please make the bad people good; and the good people nice.'! How can you make sure that your 'after' is a good advertisement for Jesus?

DAY 20: COUNT YOUR BLESSINGS

Count your blessings: name them one by one, Count your blessings: see what God has done; ...And it will surprise you what the Lord has done.

This sentimental old song encourages us to reflect on what God *has* done for us. Take time out to do this.

Colossians 1:24-29

'I am glad...' (24). Writing from prison, Paul still bubbles over with things which make him happy:

❍ His experience of suffering (24), which accompanied his work for the church (see Acts 9:15,16, part of the story of his conversion) and brought him closer to Christ. Yet he is not a masochist enjoying suffering for its own sake.

❍ The privilege God has given him in making him a servant of the gospel (25).

❍ The word of God, the message of the gospel (25,26), formerly kept secret, now explained.

❍ Christ's presence in his friends and their confident 'hope of sharing in God's glory' (27) after death.

How many of these apply to you in some measure?

For Paul, the natural responses to the privileges given him are:

❍ To share the message with others (28). Like him, 'the people that spread the gospel in the early church were the nameless little people — they were just chattering. They couldn't keep quiet in the wine shops, in the laundries, on the street corners...' *(Michael Green, contemporary theologian and speaker)*

❍ To work for God (29) — he toils and agonises in his task for God — with the energy God gives him.

The gospel should affect us on the level of our emotions, and be reflected in deep excitements, joys and sorrows. But it should also affect us in our motivation to serve.

THE OLD TESTAMENT STORY

The Bible comes to life when we understand the background to the words we read. What we call the 'Old Testament' of the Bible is a library of 39 books of very different types, written by many authors over a period of more than a thousand years. (In Catholic Bibles there are 46 books which include books commonly known as 'the Apocrypha' or the 'deutero-canonicals'.) The first book starts 'In the beginning…'. Unfortunately, the rest of the books are not arranged in exact chronological order. Take your Bible now and look at the 'Contents' page near the beginning.

THE MAJOR SECTIONS OF THE OLD TESTAMENT

A: GENESIS to DEUTERONOMY are known as 'The Law', though they also contain early history.

B: JOSHUA to ESTHER are the historical books, and are roughly in order.

C: JOB to SONG OF SONGS include poetry and collections of wise sayings known as 'wisdom' literature. Psalms is the Hebrew book of songs and prayers for worship, built up over a long period.

D: ISAIAH to MALACHI are the books of the prophets, God's spokesmen. They heard God's words and spoke or wrote them to his people. They are not in chronological order.

TIME CHART OF OLD TESTAMENT HISTORY

Main events & Characters	Date (BC)	Books
Creation, Fall, Flood	?	Genesis
Founding Fathers of Israel (Abraham, Isaac, Jacob [=Israel])	2000-1700	Genesis
Escape from Egypt	1280	Exodus
Wandering in the desert	1280-1240	Exodus, Numbers, Leviticus & Deuteronomy
Entry into Canaan	1240-1200	Joshua
Israel settles in	1200-1050	Judges
Samuel, Saul, David & Solomon	1050-970	1 & 2 Samuel, 1 & 2 Chronicles, Psalms, Proverbs & Ecclesiastes
Nation divided into Israel (N) and Judah (S); Prophets Elijah & Elisha	930-800	1 & 2 Kings, 2 Chronicles
Israel conquered & Judah attacked by Assyria	800-650	2 Kings, 2 Chronicles, Amos, Hosea, Isaiah
Judah conquered by Babylon, many exiled	650-538	2 Kings, 2 Chronicles, Jeremiah, Ezekiel
Return of exiles to Jerusalem	538-430	Ezra, Nehemiah, Zechariah, Malachi

SPECTATOR OR ACTIVIST?

INTRODUCTION TO READINGS 21 TO 34, IN ACTS, ISAIAH, AND MATTHEW.

Christians believe that the events of the Bible record God's actions in history ('His Story') and provide on-going guidance to believers. They are not legends or tales but can often be verified historically. God is active in history, not a distant spectator (Amos 9:7).

The narratives derive from oral and written traditions about God and humans handed down from one generation of believers to the next. This history of salvation starts with the Bible's first words, 'In the beginning, God' and ends with its last, 'I will come again'.

1. **God was active in the past**. Readings 21 to 27, in Acts chapters 3, 6, 7. God's long-term plans were worked out over the centuries.
2. **God is not bound by time**. Readings 28 to 30, in Isaiah chapter 11. In other chapters, Isaiah told how the Assyrian and Babylonian empires would conquer the northern kingdom Israel (Ephraim) and the southern kingdom Judah, respectively. Some people would be killed, many taken into exile. Chapter 11 looks more to the light at the end of the tunnel. From our point in history we can see that he foretold the return from exile and the coming of the Messiah. Each came to pass in stages, with at least one stage still to come.
3. **God has plans for the future.** Readings 31 to 34, in Matthew chapter 24. Written to help us prepare for Jesus' return, this prophecy awaits fulfilment. As with Isaiah's prophecies, believers will be able to say as each stage comes to pass, 'So *that* was what Jesus meant!', and understand that he knows what he is doing. It is easier, however to interpret backwards rather than forwards.

DAY 21: GOD IN CONTROL

If you have heard of any titles or names given to Jesus (for example, 'Emmanuel, God with us') choose one or two of them and turn them around in your mind. Ask, 'If Jesus is this, what does it mean for me?'

Acts 3:11-26

A dramatic healing miracle (1-10) draws a curious crowd. Peter seizes the chance to tell them the truth about Jesus.

He tells them some facts they know already (13-15) and one that perhaps they don't know (15).

He tells them what the facts mean: 'You had no idea what you were doing when you killed Jesus, and neither did your leaders. But God ... knew exactly what you were doing and used it to fulfil his plans.' (17,18, Eugene Peterson's paraphrase) God was in control, turning evil to good.

He backs what he says with evidence: God predicted it all long ago. The suffering servant (13,18) was foretold by Isaiah (check his prophecy in Isaiah 52:13; 53:4); the prophet 'like himself' (22) was foretold by Moses (check Deuteronomy 18:18); the descendant of Abraham (25) through whom all people would be blessed, was promised by Abraham (check Genesis 22:18)

He tells them that these facts are relevant to them here and now. They are curious about a healed paralytic, but there is a disability more serious than physical disease — human sin. The risen Jesus, the author of life who could not stay dead, was able to wipe clean the slate of the past, and give fresh strength to individuals to rise above the drudgery and world-weariness of the present (19).

What did they have to do to receive these blessings?
Have you done this?

DAY 22: BEING LIKE JESUS CAN COST YOU

O Holy Jesus, most merciful Redeemer, Friend and Brother, may I know Thee more clearly, love Thee more dearly, and follow Thee more nearly, day by day. *(Richard of Chichester, AD 1197)*

Acts 6

Residents of a graveyard do not argue (as far as we know). But members of a lively, growing church, are a different matter! Here, food distribution problems among the needy led to the appointment of seven 'deacons' to administer the program, a wise move. This left the apostles free for prayer and preaching. Compassionate service and teaching the Bible are not 'either/or' choices for any Christian or church.

One of the new leaders proved outstanding. He demonstrated:

❍ a sweet and strong character (5,8,15)

❍ the ability to perform miracles (8)

❍ great wisdom in his teaching (10)

In resembling Jesus, Stephen received similar treatment to him. Debate led to lies and lies to violence (9-12). It is easy to resort to similar tactics when we react strongly to what we hear.

We will all have opportunities to 'serve tables', working for God in unexciting ways. To do these tasks well, we need to be just as 'full of the Spirit and wisdom' (3) as when we carry out more visible kinds of service — perhaps more so. Pray that the Lord will equip you and point you towards whatever he wants you to do this week or for the longer term.

How might you respond to a verbal challenge to your faith? When someone twists your words and threatens you with violence or imprisonment? Would you go on the defensive? Curl up and cry? Get angry and strike out? Few of us look like angels when we are falsely accused (15).

DAY 23: GOD IS WITH US - WHEREVER

'He will be called Immanuel, which means "God is with us."' 'Go… I will be with you always…' (From the first and the last chapters of Matthew's gospel.)

Acts 7:1-16

Over the centuries Jewish religious leaders attempted to reduce God to a manageable size. Following him became a matter of worshipping in the temple and obeying a set of rigid rules, with practices controlled by a static, traditional priestly aristocracy. Here, Stephen gives his accusers a run-down on the history of their nation, drawing totally unexpected, and therefore shocking lessons from the familiar facts.

He begins with a description of the roots of Israel's faith and history. Abraham, for example, had no inheritance, no sacred sites, no home, no children at the time — only God's promise and presence. Similarly, Joseph was rejected by his brothers and sold as a slave to Egypt. But 'God was with him and rescued him' (9,10).

In other words, the religion of their revered founding fathers was not bound up in sacred buildings and rigid rules. We will see as we work through the themes Stephen develops in this chapter, how he challenges their complacency.

Is our relationship to God tied to:

❍ buildings: churches, or even trivial things such as a special seat in our church building?

❍ rituals: particular church services, kinds of music, or even an obsession with daily Bible reading?

❍ obeying laws: 'If I do/don't do this, God will be very pleased with me'?

These things can be good, as a means of knowing God, but not as ends in themselves. If we confine God to certain practices or places, we can prevent him from working with us in less expected ways.

DAY 24: HE GETS THINGS DONE

Think about this children's song:
Like a seed that's growing secret
in the darkness of the underground.
No-one knows it, no-one sees it,
no-one hears it growing, not a sound.
He gets things done
with a minimum of fuss he gets things done.
You may never hear the beating of his drum,
But that's the way the world is run. (Robin Mann)

Acts 7:17-29

God in control 1. Six centuries is a short time for God, even to remember a promise (17) — read about it in Genesis 15:12-14.

God in control 2. Bad people can't stop God. A change of dynasty in Egypt brought to power a new king, ignorant of history and suspicious of the growing Hebrew minority. After 400 years in Egypt the Hebrews still refused to call themselves Egyptians. Extermination seemed to be the only way to defeat them. Against the odds one baby boy survived (21) and received an education that would help him to lead his people to freedom.

God in control 3. Good people can't rush God. Moses knew whose side he was on. He thought the time had come to strike (25) but was wrong. We can be sincere in our actions, yet out of step with God's plan.

Hindsight is an exact science. Neither Moses in the desert nor Joseph in prison knew how God was going to work things out. Things appeared to have gone horribly wrong for them. Yet they waited and trusted.

Think of some of the things you have worried over. Thank God for the way they actually worked out. What can you learn from this? Think also of people in exile or in prison for their faith. Pray for them.

DAY 25: GOD USES REJECTS

Grant, Lord, the ear to hear your word,
the mind to understand,
the heart to respond.

Acts 7:30-43

God often chooses what people reject. Festo Kivengere, a great and godly Ugandan, used to say 'Moses spent forty years trying to be somebody, forty years discovering he was nobody, and forty years discovering what God could do with somebody who was nobody!'

Time and again God uses people the world has written off. Here we see Moses, rejected by his people because he acted ahead of God's plan, now sent an angel to assist him to 'rescue the people and be their leader' (35). Mary put it this way in her song of praise: He 'drags strong rulers from their thrones and puts humble people in places of power' (Luke 1:52).

Nobody understood better than Jesus this way of gentleness, of refusing to use the power that was available to him. Nobody failed more than the Jewish leaders to understand it, with tragic results.

People often reject what God has chosen. As soon as things became tough, the people rejected not only Moses but the God he stood for. The awesome 'I AM' was too uncontrollable for them. So they turned to more familiar idols, a pattern repeated throughout their history. Stephen showed this, quoting from a later prophet Amos ('you were too busy building shrines to war gods, to sex goddesses…', verse 43 in Peterson's paraphrase).

That which is Christ-like within us shall be crucified.
It shall suffer and be broken.
And that which is Christ-like within us shall rise up.
It shall love and create. *(Michael Leunig)*

Have you seen God work counter to your expectations?

DAY 26: DON'T SHOOT THE MESSENGER

From the cowardice that dares not face new truth,
the laziness content with half truths,
and the arrogance that thinks it knows all truth,
good Lord, deliver us. *(source unknown)*

Acts 7: 44-53

The defendant becomes prosecutor, and the two prongs of Stephen's argument land on target like a boxer's left-and-right punch. He spells out to the Jewish leaders that:

❍ no building can contain God — if God has any home on earth, it is with his people. If where we worship becomes more important than the God it honours, there is something wrong.

❍ they were rejecting what the Holy Spirit was trying to tell them. Just as in the past their forefathers rejected Joseph, Moses, and the prophets, now they rejected 'the Righteous One', Jesus. If they had not been so blind, they would have seen how he fulfilled their sacrifices, their law and their temple. Jesus himself was the final sufficient sacrifice (1 Peter 3:18). To love him was to fulfil the law (Galatians 5:14) and his people were themselves the new temple of God (Ephesians 2:19-21).

Stephen was really sad and angry at the way these leaders had treated Jesus, and the way their blindness turned others away from him.

The writer of Psalm 74 prayed

How much longer will our enemies sneer? Won't they ever stop insulting you? Why don't you punish them? Why are you holding back?

How do *you* feel when people show contempt for God? When they teach untruths about him ? When they lead others astray? How should you feel?

Is there something you can do to prepare yourself to speak up when these situations arise? Pray that you can say the right words then.

DAY 27: FIX YOUR EYES ON JESUS

'Make me your fuel, flame of God.'

(missionary martyr Jim Elliot)

Acts 7:54-60

The ball is at his feet, and there's no-one to beat but the goalie as he powers towards the goal. In the stands the coach leaps to his feet and ecstatically cheers him on. Is this comparison too far fetched? Jesus is normally described as 'seated' at God's right hand, but here he is *standing* (56)!

The Jewish leaders cover their ears, but they cannot completely shut out the godliness and Christ-likeness of the man before them.

Obadiah Kariuki was a gentle and courageous witness to Christ during the Mau Mau emergency in Kenya in 1952, when many Kikuyu Christians died for their faith. During a later time of pressure on Christians, Obadiah, by then a bishop, wrote 'For each one who is persecuted, there must be a personal persecutor: that direct confrontation is the chance for the Christian to give his persecutor a very, very close glimpse of the depth, strength and truth of what his faith really means to him.'

The church leader Tertullian, another African, wrote at the end of the second century AD: 'The blood of the martyrs is the seed of the church.' Saul, later to be Paul, watched Stephen die. What seeds were sown in his mind? What fruit did they later bear?

Sometimes this gracious way that God has of bringing good out of evil is described as 'The Resurrection Principle'. Can you work out why? Are there situations in your life where it might apply?

'He is no fool who gives what he cannot keep to gain what he cannot lose.'

(Jim Elliot)

P.S. Think about *your* last words. What would you like to say?

DAY 28: JESUS, SON OF DAVID

'Lord Jesus, there is no difficulty, inward or outward, which Thou art not ready to meet in me today.' *(Bishop Handley Moule)*

Isaiah 11:1-5

David, the youngest son of Jesse, lived some 300 years before Isaiah wrote this. A great king, he conquered Israel's enemies, united the tribes, set up a capital Jerusalem, that the nation could take pride in, and put in motion the building of its first temple. After the death of his son Solomon, the kingdom split into two, and over the next 700 years fell to a succession of invaders — including the Romans of Jesus' time.

In the fertile soil of this humiliation and oppression, the idea grew strongly that a second great king, like David and descended from him, would again lead Israel to freedom and fame.

This did occur, but not in the way people imagined!
That king was Jesus, and, as foretold by Isaiah,

- he was a direct descendant of David (Matthew 1)
- he was full of wisdom, knowledge and power (2)
- he delighted in serving the Father (3)
- he looked at people's hearts, not just their outward appearance. We can see this in his acceptance of many people, despised by others because of disease, occupation or race (3, see also Matthew 8:1-3; 9:9-11; John 4:4-7)
- he was given authority to judge (Acts 17:31)

Many who try to live for Jesus today are sickened and disheartened by the superficiality, foolishness, and corruption they see around them. Take heart, if you feel like this. The same Spirit (2) who rested on Jesus now comes to those who welcome him into their lives. Wisdom and knowledge, integrity and goodness are among his gifts and graces.

DAY 29: JESUS, PRINCE OF PEACE

To build anything, whether it be a house, a relationship, a character, a reputation, a society, is slow, hard, painstaking work. Sadly, to destroy is quick, easy, painful, devilish. All round the world, selfishness, deceit, vandalism, gossip, violence, arson and war demonstrate this.

Observing this can be depressing and soul-destroying for those who actually feel the pain, listening impotently to Satan's mocking laughter. But, in C.S. Lewis' words, 'all the leaves of the New Testament are rustling with the rumour that it will not always be so'.

Isaiah 11:6-9

One day, when the Prince of Peace (Isaiah 9:6) sets up 'a new heaven and a new earth', all of nature will be changed. But that is 'not yet'. For the time being, the Prince *has* founded a new society, designed to be a foretaste of the new world in store for us. In it, ideally:

❍ enemies become friends: we were like enemies of God, living our lives in contempt of his laws and his offer of love. But now we are reconciled to him. And we can be reconciled to earthly enemies too (Ephesians 2:14-18), something as remarkable as a wolf and a sheep lying down together!

❍ the strong and the weak live in peace: Jesus showed how strength can be used to defend the weak rather than to exploit them.

Lord, make me an instrument of your peace.
Where there is hatred, let me sow love,
Where there is injury, pardon,
Where there is doubt, faith,
Where there is despair, hope,
Where there is darkness, light,
Where there is sadness, joy.

(based on the words of St Francis of Assisi)

DAY 30: JESUS, LORD OF ALL

'What makes us greater than other nations? We have a God who is close to us and answers our prayers.' (Deuteronomy 4:7)

Isaiah 11:10-34

In this section Isaiah looks forward to

- the return of the faithful survivors of the two kingdoms (11,12)
- their being reconciled as one nation again

These prophecies were fulfilled, partly at least, in the 6th century BC and following centuries: the exiles returned, and the nation was re-formed. But, much more briefly, Isaiah hints at a far more widespread rescue operation, which was, and still is being fulfilled — in Jesus.

Not just Israel, but 'the nations', will gather to give honour to this descendant of David (10, see Reading 28). Jesus, Son of David, will be 'a signal'. Just as soldiers in battle found strength and unity rallying to a Roman eagle or a regimental flag, so people of all nations, drawn to Jesus (see John 12:32), will come together as God's new society, the church.

Our God, who is timeless, was able to give Isaiah these words to write, because every moment of past, present and future time is NOW to him.

Is there a time in your past that hangs around your memory like an unpleasant smell? Ask God to go back there with you to deal with it, to set you free from the fear or shame or guilt.

Is there a time in your future that hangs over you — a decision to be made, a danger or a judgement to be faced? God is there already, waiting for you. Trust him.

Remember and take comfort that he is here now, with you. Nothing is too trivial, too embarrassing or too frightening to share, in past or future.

DAY 31: THE END WILL COME

If you knew you had only six months to live, what difference would this make to you? Or, if you knew the world would end in six months?

Matthew 24:1-14

The return or second coming of the Lord Jesus, is a topic many Christians avoid. Why so?
❍ Many of the prophecies are hard to understand ❍ Christians are embarrassed by the wild claims and predictions of some Christian leaders ❍ The ideas smack too much of the supernatural to fit easily with contemporary materialistic thinking. Can we entertain the idea of a total end to this solid world? God step into history? Unthinkable!

Nevertheless, there are over 300 references to Jesus' return in the New Testament (about once in every 15 verses), and this reading shows how important the matter was to Jesus himself.

When the disciples commented (with national pride?) on the impressive size and beauty of the temple (1), they did not expect to receive this heavy dose of difficult teaching!

'Don't be deceived', Jesus is saying, 'don't let your faith be too dependent on a building. This one will be torn down.' The disciples seem to think this could only happen at the end of the world, so this *must* be what Jesus is talking about (3). But the temple *was* destroyed in AD 70, less than 40 years later! **'Don't be disturbed'**, Jesus is saying, 'wars and disasters (6,7) are just part of normal history.' **'Don't be disheartened'**, Jesus is saying, 'it's normal for the Christian to live with persecution and wickedness' (9,12). But 'stay with it — you won't be sorry' (13, Peterson's paraphrase).

Which of these three statements that Jesus gave to encourage us most applies to your situation at this moment?

DAY 32: DON'T HANG AROUND - RUN!

Jesus said, 'You may have peace … you will have trouble.' (John 16:33, NIV). So, trouble is certain; peace is possible. Peace is not the absence of trouble but the presence of Christ.

Matthew 24:15-28

Jesus refers to a prophecy in Daniel 11:31 — a horrible object was to be placed in the temple, to desecrate, or spoil it (15). This did happen in 167 BC. The Greek king Antiochus IV set up a pagan altar in the temple, provoking a rebellion. Jesus seems to suggest that this would happen again. In AD 70, Roman soldiers while quelling another revolt, encircled Jerusalem and set up their eagles, with images of their 'divine' emperor, in the temple. Many in the Jerusalem church at the time, remembering what Jesus had said, fled and survived the massacre.

Jesus warns them again not to be deceived by men claiming to be the Messiah. When the Son of Man comes, no one will have to go out searching for him, he will be recognised by everyone! (27)

Our Lord is coming! Imagine meeting him. Will you run and dance, or cringe and hide?

Jesus said, 'Don't be ashamed of me and my message among these unfaithful and sinful people! If you are, the Son of Man will be ashamed of you when he comes in the glory of his Father…' (Mark 8:38).

The much-persecuted Chinese house-church leader Wang Mingdao has said: 'Shall we — in order to save our faces — be ashamed of Him and His words? … For people like this it will hardly be necessary for the Lord Jesus to be ashamed of them. They will be greatly ashamed of themselves, and will have no "face" to meet the Lord.'

DAY 33: THIS WORLD IS NOT MY HOME

'Help me to understand your Law; I promise to obey it with all my heart.' (Psalm 119:34)

Matthew 24:29-35

What can we make of verse 34? C.S. Lewis described it as 'the most embarrassing verse in the Bible.' Jesus seems to be saying that some of the people present with him will still be alive when he returns. Did he get it wrong? It is strange he should say something as definite as this, yet admit a few words later (36) that even he did not know when he would return. Or is he talking about the destruction of Jerusalem? If so, did Matthew get it wrong? Have we got it wrong?

In this type of situation we should:

❍ note with thanks the things we *can* be sure of, which are usually far more important than what we are worrying about

❍ be content to understand *when* we get to heaven (1 Corinthians 13:12)

'Most people are bothered by those passages in Scripture which they cannot understand; but … the passages in Scripture which trouble me most are those I do understand.' *(Mark Twain)*

'You have been raised to life with Christ. Now set your heart on what is in heaven, where Christ rules… Christ gives meaning to your life, and when he appears, you will also appear with him in glory.' (Colossians 3:1,4) Heaven is where you belong, but for now you live on earth. What things should begin to have priority in your life now, so they can be taken with you into the next life? (Think godliness of character, think relationships.) Remember, it's worth preparing well for the long haul — it takes time to 'become' the person God created you to be.

DAY 34: HOW SHOULD WE THEN LIVE?

'The Lord isn't slow about keeping his promises... The day of the Lord's return will surprise us like a thief. The heavens will disappear... Everything will be destroyed. So you should serve and honour God by the way you live.' (2 Peter 3:9-11)

Matthew 24:36-51

God gives each of us *some* responsibility for other people. We are accountable to Jesus for the way we do the work God has given us and how we treat the people entrusted to our care (45 onwards). When we die or when Jesus comes, whichever is first, he is going to ask us to give an account of our actions.

The parable also contains a message of hope for people whose lives bear similarities to the situation of the poor servants beaten up by the person in charge (49). If you have had 'the thick end of the stick' in your life, the teaching of the New Testament gives you sure hope that wrongs *will* be put right. The violent, the greedy, the cheat, the self-centred, the tyrant (of nation, home or workplace), those who appear to die unrepentant yet at peace, all will receive what they deserve from one who is totally just and fair. These will be treated no less fairly than those whose lives of love for God and neighbour go unrewarded on earth. Jesus *is* Lord ... and every knee *shall* bow to him!

Was there anything you did yesterday, or plan to do today or tomorrow, that you would be uncomfortable to be found doing if Jesus dropped by to see you? Would you be able to tell him your reasons for doing them? What things could you happily share with him?

USING FOOTHOLD IN A GROUP

'There are two things we cannot do alone: one is to be married and the other is to be a Christian' *(Paul Tournier)*. If you are trying to be a Christian on your own, you're doing it the hard way. Share your journey with others.

First find a good church where the worship and fellowship are Christ-centred and the teaching helps you to understand the Bible's message. It's a great 'plus' when you also feel at ease with the style of worship. If there is no local church, find a small group of Christians with whom to study the Bible, pray and mutually support. Your church may have some small groups, but otherwise, find a friend or two, introduce them to *Foothold*, and suggest you meet to discuss what you are reading. You may feel low on Bible knowledge or on leadership skills, but 'if a thing's worth doing, it's worth doing badly!' *(G.K. Chesterton)*, meaning it's still worth doing even if you can't do it as well as you'd like.

There are lots of good resources for study, but for a start try linking together personal Bible reading and group discussion. Listed below are passages dealing with the same ideas as the sections in *Foothold*. You can use the ones in column A, which are selected from the individual readings, or you can approach each theme from a fresh point of view with the passages in column B.

SECTION	**THEME**	**A**	**B**
Intro	The God who speaks	Ps 19:1-11	2 Tim 3:12-17
A	God the Creator	Gen 1:1-31	Acts 17:22-31
B	God's nature seen in Jesus	Col 1:15-20	John 1:1-18
C	The God of history	Acts 3:11-23	2 Pet 3:3-14
D	The God who directs nations	Ex 14:5-31	Deut 6:20-end; 7:17-end
E	The God who cares for people	Luke 15:11-24	Matt 11:25-12:14
F	The holiness and mercy of God	Isa 6:1-8; Judg 2:6-23	Matt 18:21-35; Rom 3:21-26
G	The God who leads	Psalm 23	Proverbs 2
H	The God who champions the oppressed	Isa 1:10-20	Psalm 10
I	The God who always loves	Ps 103:1-18; 1 John 4:7-12	Ps 34:1-14; Luke 6:27-36
J	The God who stays close	John 15:1-17	Heb 4:12-16

Some Ways to Go

One simple way is for everyone to study the passage beforehand, meet, pray, read again and then share what comes to mind — ideas, feelings, questions, doubts, and so on. This works well if the group is small and members are willing and able to learn and contribute fairly equally. However, most groups find that thinking and sharing improves if one person prepares a few questions and leads the study. This task can be rotated from week to week.

Preparing a Study

❍ Pray for God's help for yourself and the group.

❍ Divide the passage into sections, and outline the main ideas in each section.

❍ Work out questions for each section such as:

'What does it say?' (for example, in Psalm 103, pick out some things God does for us). Avoid obvious questions. If the section is uncomplicated you may not need this question.
'What does it mean?' (for example, on Luke 15, how do you think the Pharisees would have reacted to Jesus describing God as a waiting father? Why do you think the writer included this story?) What is this story saying to you now? Does it tell you something about God, about yourselves, your world or your relationships?
'How do you feel about it?' It can be good to lead the discussion out of the 'head' area and into the realm of the heart. Are any of the characteristics of God mentioned in Psalm 103 real to you?
'How should you respond?' What are you going to do about this? What could you take note of or draw encouragement from? Remember that Scripture is always seeking a response from us.

❍ At the beginning of the study use a song, a picture, a newspaper item or general question to start people thinking about the main theme.
❍ Use open ended questions rather than implying the answer is obvious,

for example, 'What reasons does Paul give?' is better than 'What three reasons does Paul give?'

❍ Avoid leading questions like, 'We don't need to worry about... do we?'

❍ If the answer is *not* in the passage, phrase your question so that people don't search in vain, then stare dumbly at their Bibles for what is not there! Say, 'From your experience/In your opinion, do people ...?'

LEADING THE STUDY

❍ Make people welcome.

❍ Produce a 'starter' item or question.

❍ Invite someone to pray, or do it yourself.

❍ Ask one or more people to read the Bible passage or the first section if it's a long one.

❍ Use prepared 'launching questions'. Listen carefully to people's contributions, and encourage others to do the same. With a larger (6+) group, occasionally divide into twos or threes for discussion and then come together to compare ideas.

❍ Throw in some 'guiding questions', such as: 'Can you explain that a bit further?', 'Can you give an example?', 'How do you feel about that?', etc.

❍ Encourage everyone to take part but be sensitive to any who may wish to remain quiet.

❍ Complete a section, summarise, then move on.

❍ Keep an eye on the clock and finish on time. Leave out questions as necessary.

❍ Take time to share news and needs for prayer, emotional support and practical help.

❍ Pray together. Encourage people to pray simply, to pray for each other, and to 'pray in' the lessons learned in the study.

❍ Ask and expect God to teach you and challenge you, through the Bible and through each other.

Checkpoint D

THE GOD WHO CARES FOR NATIONS

INTRODUCTION TO READINGS 35 TO 41, IN EXODUS AND JONAH.

GOD CARES FOR HIS PEOPLE

'God so loved the world…' Giving humans freedom was a risk God took. Soon, relations between him and us soured, as the story of the garden of Eden tells. His option was to create a nation who would become his people, and he would be their God (Exodus 6:7).

As we saw in Reading 25, the rescue of Israel from Egypt was an important part of the character-forming experience of this nation. Confucius observed how much easier and less painful it was to learn from others' mistakes than our own! But do we?

GOD CARES FOR A PAGAN CITY

One of God's purposes for this special nation was that they should be a means of sharing his blessing with all the other peoples of the earth (Genesis 12:1-3). The message of Jonah is a reminder of this high privilege, which Israel constantly failed to accept.

From many passages in the New Testament (such as 1 Peter 2:9-10) it is clear that both these privileges — of being God's chosen people, and of 'declaring his praises' — now belong to the church.

Each section contains a major problem. These quotes from present-day Old Testament scholars may help to keep these manageable.

❍ ***The drowning of the Egyptians*** (Exodus 15:9-10). 'There are moments when judgement takes precedence over long-suffering. Wrath is not first nature to God. But it is a part of his nature. He is not soft over evil.' *(John Goldingay)*

❍ ***The great fish, or whale*** (Jonah 1). 'It is possible to interpret the book either as history or as parable.' *(John B. Taylor)* Either way, it doesn't destroy the authority of the Bible.

DAY 35: HE IS MY GOD, I WILL PRAISE HIM

'Worship is the submission of all our nature to God. It is the quickening of conscience by His holiness; the nourishment of mind with His truth; the purifying of imagination by His beauty; the opening of the heart to His love; the surrender of will to His purpose.' *(William Temple)*

Exodus 15:1-10

This song celebrates the nation's dramatic rescue from a desperate situation, where the untrained and lightly armed people of Israel were trapped between the Red Sea and a powerful Egyptian army. Read about it in chapter 14. Like the song, most worship celebrates both what God *is* in himself, and what he *has done* for us.

God is a warrior. He was, and is, permanently at war with every form of evil (3). The war is not yet over. But our God is on our side, fighting for us against all that would enslave or diminish us.

God has acted decisively. In Jesus, on the Cross, he has fought and won a far greater victory over a much more deadly enemy, Satan. By adopting us as his new people, he has swept us up into this victory and has become our salvation (2).

Though occurring in far different situations, nearly all the promises and privileges given to the 'People of God' in the Old Testament are, in the New Testament, applied to the church. Has God set you free from a kind of slavery? Are you captive to something which needs to be worked on? Pick out the 'I' and 'my' statements (1,2) and make them your own. Worship God. Trust him. Find ways to ensure recognition and praise is given to God for what he continues to do in your church.

DAY 36: OUR GOD REIGNS

Think about God. Write down two words that come to mind

______________________ ; ______________________ .

Think about yourself. Write down two words that come to you

______________________ ; ______________________ .

Now write a simple prayer of your own, weaving all four words into, for example, a 'thankyou' prayer, a 'sorry' prayer, or a 'please' prayer.

Exodus 15:11-21

Moses and the Israel Choral Society move on from what God *has* done to what he *will* do. When we see God working, our faith in him grows. At the bottom of these pages, start keeping note of answered prayers and other instances of his hand as they occur. They are easily forgotten (Satan works hard on this).

'Redeemed' (13, NIV; 'rescued', CEV) is a power-packed word. Literally, it means 'bought back' (like an object reclaimed from a pawn-shop) but in the culture of the times it had a much fuller meaning. Then, if you were foolish enough to get into debt, you could be forced to sell yourself as a slave to pay it off. Your nearest relative was then honour-bound to buy you out (redeem you), if he was able. If you were murdered, it was up to him to avenge you, and marry your widow. Imagine what must have passed through the mind of Moses when God promised to become such a 'redeemer-relative' for him and the whole nation of Israel (Exodus 6:6).

'...our great God and Saviour, Jesus Christ... gave himself for us to redeem us from all wickedness and to purify for himself a people that are his very own...' (Titus 2:13-14, NIV). Would you describe yourself as being one of Jesus' 'own people' yet? How far along the 'redeeming' process have you come?

DAY 37: WHY PRAY WHEN YOU CAN GRUMBLE?

How do you *feel*? Does God seem near, or far away? The great Baptist preacher (and pray-er) Charles Spurgeon said, 'We should pray when we are in a praying mood, for it would be sinful to neglect so fair an opportunity. We should pray when we are not in a praying mood, for it would be dangerous to remain in so unhealthy a condition.'

Exodus 15:22-27

In the space of an unforgettable few days the Israelites went through three kinds of experience: the *dangers* (and triumphs) of the Red Sea 'high', followed quickly by the *disappointments* of the Marah 'low'. Then came the *delights* of the Elim peace and rest.

Each of these situations, for us as well as them, has the potential for disaster. But each is also an opportunity for learning, which is why God allows things like this to take place.

The wilderness East of Suez is impressive, but hostile. Here, after three days of walking, the Israelites' reaction to the bitterness of the Marah water was understandable. But what did they do wrong? And what did Moses do right?

Then Elim ('trees' in Hebrew) — after a short time in the desert, wells and trees quickly become things to dream and drool about. No wonder someone actually counted them! But judging from the next few verses (16:1,2) the Israelites found ease and prosperity as difficult to cope with as their previous disappointments and dangers.

How do you handle danger? With despair or trust? How do you handle disappointment? With grumbling or prayer? How do you handle delight or ease and prosperity? With idle self-satisfaction or praise and thanks?

DAY 38: ASLEEP IN THE STORM

'You have looked deep into my heart, Lord, and you know all about me. You know when I am resting or when I am working... Where could I go to escape from your Spirit or from your sight?' (Psalm 139:1,2,7) Do you sometimes feel like running away from God? Why?

Jonah 1

'Jonah, go to Nineveh. Tell them to repent of their savageness, before I punish them for it.'

'But Lord; they're idolatrous pagans; we Jews are supposed to keep ourselves separate.' 'Jonah, **go**!' 'But Lord! They're ruthless, bloodthirsty ... I might get ... you know ...' 'Jonah, go!' 'But Lord, they're disgusting, they're different — what if they want to become Jews?' 'Jonah, **GO!!'**

So Jonah went. (But in the opposite direction.)

Lessons that Jonah may or may not have learned:

❍ You can't get away from God.

❍ People who aren't 'officially' God's people can also understand how he works (10,14).

❍ The first step to a fresh start is... (12)

Is this a fair picture? Outside in the world, there are storms raging: violence and immorality in society and in the family, cyclones of poverty and corruption, winds of aggressive anti-Christian attitudes, floods of seductive materialism, droughts of terrible emptiness of heart.

Inside our safe churches, many Christians are asleep, hiding, enjoying our great privileges but indifferent to our huge responsibilities to society.

We too cannot hide from God. It is *to Christians* that Peter says, 'But you are God's chosen and special people. You are a group of royal priests and a holy nation. God has brought you out of darkness into his marvellous light.' (1 Peter 2:9) Does this give you any fresh insights into your situation?

DAY 39: DEEP WATER MOMENTS

'God whispers to us in our pleasures, speaks in our conscience, but shouts in our pains.' *(C.S. Lewis)* Lord, I'm not very good at listening to you. I hope you won't have to shout.

Jonah 2

Hebrews were terrified of the sea — it symbolised all that was evil and uncontrollable in the world. No wonder Jonah felt rescued already when he'd only got as far as the fish's belly! (6)

His situation depicts our 'deep water moments' (DWM's) when we realise that we don't have life under control, that there are forces within us and outside us that we can't deal with by ourselves. Like Jonah, we can learn that :

❍ DWM's *can* happen to God's people: being a Christian is not a kind of vaccination that makes us immune to all fear and trouble.

❍ DWM's *can* result from disobedience: there may be other causes, but it is wise to check our consciences to see whether the DWM is 'God shouting'.

❍ DWM's *can* be great learning times, *if* we come at them in a godly way.

When we hit a DWM, what can we be sure of?
❍ It's not worth mucking about with God (4)
❍ Whatever happens, God is still on our side (6)

A competition for paintings with the title 'Peace' brought in the expected pictures of lakes, valleys, sunsets, etc. One gave a better picture of what God's peace (Philippians 4:6,7) can be for us. It showed a branch of a tree in a thunderstorm: in the branch was a nest, and in the nest, under its mother's wing, was a baby bird.

Do you know anyone going through a DWM? What specific prayers can you pray for them? For yourself?

DAY 40: GOD CARED - GOD SENT

Father, because we needed forgiveness, you sent Jesus into the world to live and teach and die and rise again. Because I needed forgiveness you sent someone to tell me about him. Thankyou. From my often ungrateful heart, thankyou!

Jonah 3:1-10

Some reassuring things to learn about God:
From Jonah. Failure is not trivial — it can be a costly business for both God and us (and perhaps for others) — *but* neither is failure final. God does not tell Jonah to get lost, he just quietly gives him his orders again. Moses, Peter, and many others have made mistakes and each has made the same refreshing discovery about what it means to work for God.
From Nineveh. In our very individualistic 'what's in it for me' society it is good to be reminded that God cared for Nineveh as a community (see 4:11). Our communities and nations too are corporately subject to God's judgement, and corporately capable of repentance and renewal. They are deeply in need of both.

'Christianity which does not begin with the individual, does not begin; but Christianity which ends with the individual, ends.' *(David Bosch)*

God cared for the people of Nineveh, enough to send Jonah to them. When Jesus saw the crowds, 'he felt sorry for them. They were confused and helpless, like sheep without a shepherd'. (Matthew 9:36-38) So he sent his disciples out. Maybe someone you know is in need of an understanding friend. Reflect for a time on those around you and pray for them. Or is there a group of people further away from you who could use your assistance. Is Jesus wanting to use you, as he once sent someone to you? Ask him.

DAY 41: MANIC MOOD SWINGS

'To become a Christian is to encounter the reality of God; to become a disciple is to allow this encounter to shape the way in which we think — and act.' *(Alister McGrath)*
Lord, shape my thinking and my living today.

Jonah 4

Verses 1-3:

❍ Correct theology (2) is great, but unless there is genuine love for God and people it goes sour.

❍ God's judgement is an essential part of biblical truth, but if we find we're *enjoying the idea* that a particular group of people is condemned, or sad when they are forgiven, then we're in trouble. Abraham Lincoln, urged to take revenge, said 'Do I not destroy my enemies when I make them my friends?'

Verses 4-8:

❍ Violent mood swings like Jonah's are typical of superficial Christians who enjoy God only for what he gives, and not for what he is.

'I love you, Not only for what you are,
But for what I am When I am with you…
And for what you are making of me.' *(from a love poem, source unknown)*

Verses 9-11:

❍ Jonah's anger may have been fed by self-pity ('I must have looked a fool'), by his racist pride, or even his tiredness.

❍ When you feel angry with God it is much better to talk it out than to walk out. Jonah does this — and God can cope (see Job 3:11-17).

❍ Think of a group of people you find easy to fear or hate, or to whom you feel superior. Suppose half a dozen of them joined your church — how would you react?

Have any of the comments above found the mark with you? Turn them into prayers.

HOW WE GOT OUR NEW TESTAMENT

Christians have always been 'people of the book'. The early believers had only the Old Testament, but they prized it greatly. It told of how God had rescued a people and prepared them for himself. More, it contained God's word, his message to his people. It embodied God's law. Supremely, it pointed forward to God's Son.

Like all Jews, the first Christians were quite clear that God had revealed himself in that book. They were clear that Jesus was the climax and crown of the gradual unfolding of God's revelation in the Old Testament. So wherever they went they used the Old Testament writings to explain who Jesus was and what he had achieved.

The Old Testament was the root, and Jesus the fruit, of God's plan to show himself fully to people.

Very soon the earliest missionaries were carrying with them copies of the words of Jesus, and the stories of his wonderful life, death, and resurrection. Naturally these began to be set alongside the sacred books of the Old Testament, as were the writings of his closest followers. He had called them apostles — men with mission — and their task was to draw out for future generations the meaning of his teaching, his life, his death.

Within a comparatively short time the Gospels and letters of the New Testament were combined with the Old Testament to become the book for believers. As St Augustine put it, 'The Christ who is concealed in the Old Testament is revealed in the New'.

The Bible is still a living book and God speaks to us through it. Christians continue to read it in private, in church and in small groups, finding it guides and strengthens them in everyday life.

Check point E

THE GOD WHO CARES FOR PEOPLE

INTRODUCTION TO READINGS 42 TO 48, IN JOHN'S AND LUKE'S GOSPELS.

We've seen something of the God who speaks, God the Creator, God's nature revealed in Jesus, the Lord of history and the God who cares for nations. We've also seen how each of these themes relates to ourselves. The next seven readings show more clearly how much God cares for us as individuals, welcoming us when we come to him, moving out to look for us even when we are indifferent. This can be cheering or unnerving, depending on how we see him!

We begin with Jesus' encounter with a Samaritan woman. Though the Samaritans worshipped the same God, waited for a messiah and accepted the first five books of the Old Testament as scripture, they were despised by the Jews, mostly because of ethnic tensions arising from their past. These became worse when they built their own temple on Mount Gerizim.

The woman seems strikingly modern: what emptiness of heart drove her to look for satisfaction in one partner after another? How had she reached the point where she would go alone to a well outside the town in the heat of the day, rather than face other women at the normal times?

We move to the parables in Luke 15, where Jesus describes the priority God gives to the insignificant, the weak and the lost.

Each of the 'lost' characters in the three stories has a different level of involvement: the coin is completely passive, the lamb nearly so, while the son has to get up and walk. Of course, he can do this only because he knows what kind of father he has. We may like to compare these to our own experience of rescue by God.

DAY 42: WHAT DRIVES YOU?

'As a deer gets thirsty for streams of water, I truly am thirsty for you my God. In my heart, I am thirsty for you, the living God.' If you're feeling low read the rest of Psalm 42.

John 4:1-15

Peer group expectations influence us all, but we don't like admitting it!

In the Jewish culture of Jesus' time:

❍ a man would not talk in public to a woman

❍ a Jew would not talk to any Samaritan (9); strict Jews travelling from southern Judea to northern Galilee would walk an extra three days to avoid passing through Samaria

❍ a Rabbi (religious teacher) would *never* talk to a woman he knew was immoral (Luke 7:39)

But for Jesus, the need of a lonely, thirsty woman mattered more than the opinion of others. He spoke with her as a fellow human, neither patronising nor condemning: 'Phew, I'm tired — give us a drink of water, would you?'

Water. Because we have the luxury of pure water on tap it's hard to grasp the power of this Biblical image. Not for us the weary, uphill walk from some distant stagnant pool, rationing out water for drinking, washing, etc. A cool spring that *never* runs dry? The thread runs through the Old Testament — trees growing by the water that need not fear the heat... You shall be like a well watered garden... Come, all you who are thirsty, come to the waters...

Put yourself in the place of this troubled woman with an unquenched thirst for something that will satisfy. What is this stranger trying to tell you?

This is our God. He comes to us. He takes us as we are. He talks to us. He cares. He waits.

DAY 43: SECRETS REVEALED

God doesn't *need* our worship; but he does desire it, if it is true worship: '…true worshippers are being led by the Spirit to worship the Father according to the truth. These are the ones the Father is seeking to worship him.' (John 4:23)

John 4:16-26

'Why, it was as if he lowered
a pail into the well of my soul
and brought it back brimming with secrets.'

(a poem about this story by Andrew Lansdown, in his collection, 'Windfalls'.)

None of us likes having our secrets exposed. It's not surprising the woman changed the subject. Jesus didn't give up. Bit by bit, he continued to reveal *his* secrets. He then entrusted to her the mystery that, should she grasp it, was both the theological answer to her tired intellectual arguments (20) and the personal answer to her restless search for satisfaction (18). Jesus himself is the truth, the way to God (24-26).

We can't hide anything from Jesus, but we don't have to. He knows everything, and is ready to forgive every sin and heal every wound. Having begun to trust God, can you assist others to do the same? Note the love and skill with which Jesus leads this woman to a fresh start in life:

- ❍ Though tired (7) he makes the effort
- ❍ He sparks the woman's curiosity (10,13,14)
- ❍ He takes her seriously (21)
- ❍ He explains things clearly (21-24)
- ❍ He is willing to confront her (17,18)
- ❍ He persists in spite of her evasion (20)

Does this list give you clues about how to talk to people about Jesus? How might you approach conversations with people who are open to learning more about our Lord?

DAY 44: FLOWING SPRING OR STAGNANT POOL?

Light a candle and spend a few minutes thinking about these words: 'It is the very nature of Christianity that truly to possess it inevitably leads to passing it on.' *(William Temple)*

John 4:27-42

1. Jesus met a thirsty woman. What he offered her, however, not only filled her emptiness but overflowed. The woman, with disarming simplicity, introduced others to him (29,39). Compare John 7:37-39.

2. The psychologist Abraham Maslow theorised that we respond to needs in order of importance. The most fundamental are the biological and survival needs, followed by love and self-esteem. Only then come the more sophisticated ones (religion?). For Jesus, however, there was a motivation deeper even than biological needs (34). What was it?

3. Excited with the woman's response, Jesus urges his friends (35,36) to see people as ready for 'harvesting', and themselves as reapers gathering them in to God's kingdom. (Note: verse 38 may refer to John the Baptist as Aenon was not far away. See 3:23.)

(The numbers correspond to 1-3 above)

1. What are you doing with what you know of Christ? Are you overflowing (sharing) or stagnating (keeping it to yourself)? 'Unused truth becomes as useless as an unused muscle.' *(A.W. Tozer)*

2. Write down some things you know or suspect are God's will for you: some will be general (be more like Jesus) and some specific. What priority do you give them?

3. God must sometimes look down sadly and say: 'My house is full; my fields are empty.' How's your field?

Only one life 'Twill soon be past;
Only what's done For Jesus will last. (Anon.)

DAY 45: RESPECTABLE OR RABBLE?

'What a man (or woman) is before God, that (s)he is, and no more.' *(St Francis of Assisi)* Lord, help me to see people as you see them.

Spend time thinking about some of the people you see everyday, especially those easy to overlook.

Luke 15:1-7

As we often find in the gospel story, Jesus is surrounded by an *inner* circle of marginalised, 'unimportant' people, hungrily taking in his teaching, and an *outer* ring of respectable, religious people superciliously criticising him.

The story of the lost sheep focuses on the intensity of the search and the immensity of the joy.

The Search: The shepherd leaves the flock safely in the pen and goes off searching 'until he finds' the lost one. What clue does this give to the character of the shepherd? What sort of lengths is the shepherd prepared to go to for the welfare of his sheep? How important is a single sheep to him?

The Joy: Returning with the straggling sheep across his shoulders, the shepherd shares the news. Friends and neighbours (and other sheep?) join him in a celebration of delight.

To be able to say 'The Lord is my shepherd' is great; to be in training as an under-shepherd is an even greater joy and privilege. But to do either properly we must learn the Chief Shepherd's priorities. Yet the reality is that well over 90 per cent of the church's under-shepherds are at home looking after the 99 (the Christians, the respectable people) and fewer than 10 per cent are out on the hills looking for the 'one'? Should you be reconsidering your priorities? Who might you be overlooking close to home?

DAY 46: THE SERIOUS BUSINESS OF HEAVEN

Think back to the time when you first became aware of God, how he found you, the things and people he used, the people who prayed for you. Thank your heavenly Father for the trouble he took over you.

Luke 15:8-10

The necklace or headband of ten coins (each one worth a day's pay) might have been part of the woman's savings, or a wedding gift with sentimental as well as monetary value.

Like the sheep, and the son in the next story, the coin belonged in a particular place: people who are unaware of God are out of place in the God-given order of things. Unlike the sheep and the son, the coin was unable to contribute anything towards being found — not a bleat nor a step! Similarly, many who are 'lost' don't know or care they are 'lost' — but God does.

Luke wrote this gospel for his fellow Greek-speakers. They believed their gods, such as Zeus and Artemis, were too high and mighty to be moved by human actions. Luke is glad to record how *our* God allows himself to be saddened or delighted by the responses of those he has created for himself. 'Joy is the serious business of heaven', wrote C.S. Lewis.

Are you aware of God's priorities? When you meet people who don't seem to know or even care about his existence, has Jesus' searching love encouraged you to reach out to them? And, when you hear that a 'lost' person has been found, how do you respond? Glad, indifferent?

Is God asking you to pray for someone you see regularly? Will you allow yourself to be part of the process where God can use you to 'find' them?

DAY 47: THE WAITING FATHER

'Though you are above us all, you care for humble people, and you keep a close watch on everyone who is proud.' (Psalm 138:6). Lord, help me to deal with my pride, and the many ways it disguises itself.

Luke 15:11-24

Part of the power of this timeless story lies in the tension between the characters: the actions of the crass and selfish younger son, and those of the extravagantly generous and forgiving father, both equally shocking to Jesus' listeners.

The younger son does what no Jewish son would ever do — he ignores his responsibility to care for his parents and demands his share of the inheritance, now. Life is fun — till the money runs out. What to do? He has disgraced his family, forfeited his inheritance, alienated himself from everyone that matters. Driven by hunger (remember Maslow, in Reading 44?) to take the most menial of jobs, he comes to his senses. He has no claim on his father, but could he, perhaps, ask to be taken on as a servant? Servants at least have food.

The father does what no Jewish father would ever do — he watches for his son's return. Seeing him, he gathers up his robe and, with scandalous unconcern for dignity, *runs* to meet his son. No wonder the son is unable to finish his prepared speech.

Would you believe that Jesus told this story to show what God is like? God *is* like this — to people who have reached that 'pigsty moment', admitting their failure and need. To the proud and self-sufficient God shows a very different face (see James 4:6).

Think about your everyday prayers. Are they more like the son's 'give me…' (12), or 'make me…' (19)?

DAY 48: IT'S NOT FAIR!

It is so easy to feel we are so *bad* that God wouldn't want us *or* so *good* we don't need God. Bring your insecurities and your over-confidence to God now.

Luke 15:25-32

There are thousands of fortunate people who have never known a time when they did not love Jesus. Growing up in Christian families, they have step by step come to understand that they really are children of God, accepted only by grace.

The elder son, however, is not one of these. Though outwardly he has never left home, inwardly he feels he has earned his sonship and deserves his reward. His response to his brother ('this other son of yours') shows clearly how, in his heart, he is just as much in a 'foreign country' as his brother ever was.

This is the lesson Jesus is trying to teach the religious leaders (2). In their own minds at least, they don't need to turn back to God (7). Sadly, this lesson is still relevant today.

Is God not fair then? Do we not get what we deserve? No, thank God! We'd all of us be in trouble if we did (Romans 3:20-24).

As God sees you, where are you?

❍ never left home, enjoying the warmth of the family, welcoming others who turn to God?

❍ living a good life, going to church, but inwardly feeling you have a right to God's approval?

❍ in the far country, still spending your inheritance, despising your place in the family?

❍ in the pigsty, willing to come back to your Father with empty hands, trusting in his love alone?

❍ back home, and rejoicing!

RESPONDING TO GOD'S WORD

'These two words, know and do, occur throughout Scripture, and always in that order. We cannot do until we know, but we can know without doing. The house built on the rock is the house of the man who knows and does. The house built on the sand is the house of the man who knows but does not do.' *(Francis Schaeffer)*

James, in the New Testament letter which bears his name, tells us to 'be doers of the word'. This is hard. That is why every reading in *Foothold* ends with a suggestion on how we can 'do' what we have read, practise what it teaches and allow it to sink into our hearts and minds until our desires and values, actions and ideas are in tune with it.

How is it possible to do this? British preacher, John Stott suggests five ways:

❍ 'We respond to truth about God with **worship**.' As we know God better we see more clearly how much he deserves our devotion, and respond to him through praise.

❍ 'We respond to truth about ourselves with **repentance.**' On seeing what we are like, we can turn to God to say we are sorry. Then, as forgiven people, we ask for assistance to live in tune with God's plans.

❍ 'We respond to God's promises and his reliability with **faith**.' As we learn more about God, we believe, and respond to his faithfulness.

❍ 'We respond to his authority and his commands with **obedience**.' This is how we show Jesus we love him.

❍ God has revealed his secrets to us, so we need to respond 'with **witness'**, sharing our knowledge of Jesus and our experience of him in our lives, with those who have not had this opportunity.

Checkpoint F

GOD: KIND AND STERN

INTRODUCTION TO READINGS 49 TO 62, IN ISAIAH, JUDGES AND JOHN'S GOSPEL.

Our tiny human minds cannot grasp all the different sides of God's character, although he has encouraged us to try! Two aspects of God's nature that seem to contradict each other are his *kindness* (mercy, love) and his *sternness* (holiness, justice, judgement, anger).

Some people solve the problem by playing down one or the other. Many preachers in the past went overboard on hell-fire, but today much preaching, and nearly all Christian songs, focus so strongly on God's love that his holiness is almost out of the picture. Charles Simeon summed it up 200 years ago: 'Truth is not in the middle, and not in one extreme, but in both extremes.'

To an Israelite, to be in the presence of God was as fearful and dangerous as walking unprotected into the reactor core of a nuclear power station today. Isaiah describes what God's burning purity meant for him. The vision happened at the end of the long and prosperous reign of King Uzziah, about 740 BC. Things were good on the surface, but the root of faithfulness to God was already rotting.

Then we go back to about 1200 BC, to the beginning of the 200-year-long era of the 'Judges'. This chaotic period after Israel's settlement of Canaan, showed the twelve tribes constantly under attack from surrounding nations, with as yet little sense of unity. In this period, it is really only God who is the judge: the so-called 'judges' were more like guerilla leaders.

Finally we come to the place where the paradox of God's love and justice is most fully resolved, the Cross of Christ, movingly described by John.

DAY 49: THE LONGEST JOURNEY

Are you feeling upset or anxious? Put on some quiet music and pour out your troubles to your holy Father who is not too remote to share your ups and downs.

Isaiah 6:1-7

Depressed by the death of the good king Uzziah, by the growing perversion, drunkenness and corruption of the world he lived in (see 5:20-23), Isaiah goes into the temple - and is found by God.

As always, in the effort to describe God and heaven, language struggles upward and falls back defeated: thrones and robes and smoke float across the picture, but the reality is beyond words.

The God Isaiah saw *filled* the temple: there was room for no other, except for the heavenly creatures who worshipped and served him.

To feel totally enveloped by God's presence — something longed and striven for by mystics for thousands of years — would be a delight, surely? To reach total self-awareness — the goal of any number of religious techniques, meditation, drugs, etc. — would be equally fulfilling, surely? What does Isaiah say (5)?

The longest journey, said UN Secretary General Dag Hammarskjold, is the journey inward. In the overwhelming presence of God, Isaiah makes this journey. At the centre of himself he finds, not the famous prophet, not the friend of kings, but a human being, as wretched and sinful as the rest of his people.

But it doesn't end there. God takes the initiative: the awful gulf between humans and God is crossed (from the other side), the burning coal touches, and forgiveness is his — not cheap, but free.

In *your* journey inward, where are you now? If you want a measure of how close you are to God, a good one is how conscious you are of sin.

DAY 50: BE THOU MY VISION

Master speak! and make me ready, When Thy voice is truly heard, With obedience glad and steady, Still to follow every word. I am listening, Lord, for Thee: Master, speak, oh speak to me!

(Frances Havergal)

Isaiah 6:8-13

Isaiah now hears (or rather overhears), not just the heavenly shining ones, but the Lord himself, who asks, 'Will someone go for us?'

With no job description, but content to know who the Manager is, Isaiah volunteers. Then God drops the bombshell: his message of judgement must be told but the people will not understand it or consider its message (9,10). In Old Testament thinking, God's prior knowledge of an event was understood to have also caused the event. This is a mysterious concept, but there is nothing mysterious about what happens when people continually reject a plain warning from God: their hearts become hardened to the point of no return.

'How long?' is more a cry for Isaiah's doomed nation than for himself. But there is a ray of hope (13) — just as a stump of a tree can regenerate, so will Judah. This did occur with the renewal of the Israelite nation and more fully with the birth of Christ (see 11:1-4).

Throughout his long, hard life and ministry, Isaiah's vision of God determined his concept of God. It became the 'still centre' for his strength. HE was the one Sovereign Lord, and no power could compare with him. Read chapters 36 and 37 for an illustration of how this worked out.

Think of any you know who are working for God in hard places: pray that God will renew their vision of himself, and assure them that they are where he wants them to be.

DAY 51: NO OTHER GODS BESIDE ME

Lord, take my desire to be *informed*, and add to it a willingness to be *reformed* — and a longing to be *transformed*.

Judges 2:6-40

Verses 18,19 describe Israel's miserable cycle of 'forget God' — 'suffer' — 'cry for help' — 'be rescued' — 'enjoy peace' — 'forget God'... Today, western society seems to be well into the 'forget God' stage; the signs are that the 'suffer' stage is not far away, as God allows our neglect of him to bear its bitter fruit (Romans 3:24-31). Why is God angry (20)? 'Anger is the fluid that love bleeds when you cut it' *(C.S. Lewis)*.

The nature gods of the Canaanites, who lived alongside the Israelites, were Baals (male) and Astartes (female), respectively bloodthirsty and lustful. Their 'worship' celebrated fertility and animal human nature.

When in time, all that God had done in the Exodus faded from Israel's corporate memory, it was not surprising that some Israelites found the idea of 'when in Rome, do as Rome does' logical, even attractive. Now they were farmers, fertility was the name of the game. Perhaps Baal and the other local gods knew a bit more about fertility than Yahweh their God. Not that they left him out, of course — just covered their bets.

What matters in *your* life? Who or what do you rely on? Some people feel that God is fine for Sunday but in the real world where we live, other principles operate. If we believe this, we are no different from Israel in Canaan: the things we depend on are *our* substitute gods. God lays claim to every ambition in our lives, and he can meet every need. He is not content to be boxed in to the part labelled 'religion'.

DAY 52: YOU HAVE NOT LISTENED TO ME

Make me new, whatever the pain or the cost. 'Batter my heart, three-personed God, for you as yet but knock! Breathe, shine and seek to mend; that I may rise and stand, o'erthrow me and bend your force to break, blow, burn, and make me new.'

(16th Century poet John Donne)

Judges 6:1-21

Looking eastwards from Ophrah across the Jordan valley, Joash and Gideon would have looked nervously at the mountain pass opposite. Through this pass the Midianite and Amalekite Bedouin would pour, moving silently and efficiently on the camels (5) they had only recently learned to domesticate.

Hard to accept God was using these people to work out his purposes? Easier to shrug your shoulders bitterly and assume God had forgotten you (13)? When hard times hit, it's not easy to ask 'Lord, what do you want me to learn from this?'.

Angels, God's heavenly servants, when sent to earth with a message look like ordinary human beings until they choose to reveal their nature (21,22). This passage strongly implies that angels do not have 2-metre wings sticking out of their backs as depicted on Christmas cards!

Despite ready access to the gospel in most western societies, people generally are not listening to God (10). 'The greatest question of our time is whether man can bear to live without God.' *(historian Will Durant)* Will God have to bring us to the point where we cry out to him (6)? What might he use to do this?

If God calls you to do something, is family background or God's presence (15,16) the more important qualification? Moses was not the first (Exodus 3:11,12) nor Gideon the last to question God's choice of them. Are you?

DAY 53: HE IS OUR PEACE

'Peace!' the Lord told Gideon. 'Do not be afraid.' (23, NIV) Draw five intersecting circles, overlapping in the centre. Label them — 'Harmony', 'Wholeness', 'Well-being', 'Justice', and 'Peace'. Then in the centre write *SHALOM*. This is the Hebrew word for that rich quality of life that the Lord offered, which Gideon accepted (24). Are you in special need at this time of one of these qualities? Ask God for it.

Judges 6:22-40

Gideon probably still had butterflies in his stomach from the angel-encounter and a strong feeling that he wasn't going to be able to sidestep God's call to take the lead. Now aware that before Israel could face the enemy surrounding them, he must deal with the enemy within, *shalom* was exactly what Gideon needed.

His nervous request for further signs (36-40) is understandable but not the right way to seek God's guidance. Some Christians use this incident to justify seeking God's guidance. They make similar requests such as: 'If you want me to marry X, then please make them phone tomorrow.' The passage does not give support to this method because in view of the specific commands (14,16) and supernatural signs he received (21,28,34), Gideon's request for further signs is an expression of unbelief. The New Testament, likewise, does not support this way of seeking guidance from God (see Luke 1:18-20).

When God calls *you* to do something and you have doubts or questions about either your ability or his power, pray for courage to take the first step. Even though you are unsure how things will unfold, his Spirit will support and enable you (34). 'The Lord *is* peace.' Is he *your* peace?

DAY 54: GOD'S WORK DONE IN GOD'S WAY

'Without God we cannot; without us he will not' *(St Augustine)*. Thank you, heavenly father, that despite my inexperience, doubts, lack of faith and fears, you still find things for me to do. I thank you especially for the responsibilities you have given me: helping ________________, sharing with ________________, praying for ________________ *(fill in the names)*.

Judges 7:1-14

Imagine you're Gideon, at the point described in verse 1. Do a 'SWOT analysis' of your situation (that is, list the Strengths, Weaknesses, Opportunities and Threats that are at work). Would it matter that you're heavily outnumbered (see 7:3,12; 8:10)? How would you feel as God's further directions keep coming in (2,3 & 4-7)? And Gideon, how might God be feeling about him at this point? Does God 'hang in' with him? Does he despise his fears? Look at verses 9-14. See how God makes arrangements for Gideon to glimpse the preparations made for the way ahead (9-14).

We work hard to create ways to reduce the amount of faith in God that we need each day —locks on the door, cash in the bank, friends at the church… There is nothing wrong with these, but if we can't do without them, God may have to take away these supports from us. How would you survive if God 'did a Gideon' (7) on your money, or your friends?

Appointed director of a large mission at a time of great crisis, Frank Houghton wrote:

It is a secret joy to find; The task assigned Beyond our powers.
For then, if aught of good be wrought, Clearly the praise is His, Not ours.

Under a different kind of pressure, Paul wrote 2 Corinthians 12:10. How far can you agree with him?

DAY 55: USED FOR GOD

Shamgar had an ox-goad, David had a sling,
Dorcas had a needle, Rahab had some string.
Samson had a jawbone, Aaron had a rod,
Mary had some perfume — all were used for God. (Anon.)

(You may wish to read the stories behind the names here in Judges 3:31; 1 Samuel 17; Acts 9:36-43; Joshua 2:17-21; 6:25; Judges 15:11-16; Exodus 7:8-13; John 12:1-8.)

Lord, you have given me gifts — help me to develop them and to learn how to use them for you without being arrogant.

Judges 7:15-end

God didn't despise Gideon's fears (remember yesterday's reading) nor his considerable gifts. The planning and execution of the attack showed enormous creativity, leadership, and discipline, all bent towards the God-given task.

Like many of the leaders of his time, Gideon grasped an important lesson: if God wants you to do a job, he stands by you and helps you through, even though it may be far from easy.

Sadly, the book of Judges shows how Israel failed to learn even this lesson in any permanent way. Still more disastrously, they failed to learn that people cannot 'live as though there were a fool on the throne of the universe', and get away with it.

Gideon's story illustrates how God uses people who are willing to listen when he calls, to 'have a go' at a task that appears to be beyond their capabilities — and how life becomes much more exciting when they do!

Ask God to show you if you are too set in your ways, and in what direction he wants you to step out.

DAY 56: DIE BEFORE YOU DIE

Lord, I am glad you are with me where I am. But I also want to be with you where you are. Show me today more about what this will mean.

John 12:20-26

John, writing in his gospel, often drops clues about a much deeper pattern of ideas. Reading between the lines, can you follow Jesus' train of thought? … Greeks … salvation not for Jews only, but for all people … but before that, the Cross — very soon now … to God's eyes, glory (23) … to human eyes, plain death … but not just death, new life (24) … like a grain of wheat …

The network of ideas is so rich, a 'mind map' might help — add what other 'blobs' you can.

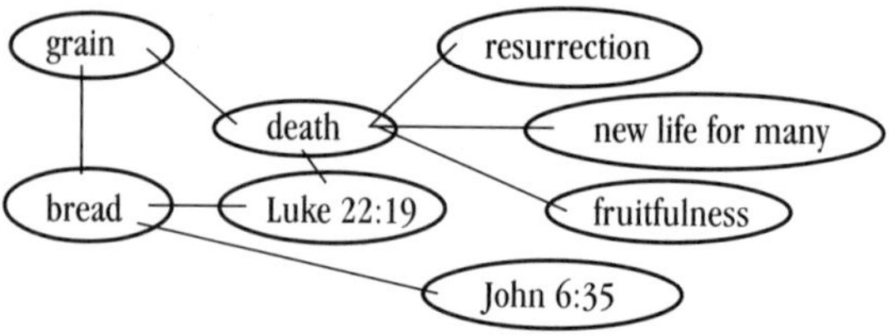

Deep inside each of us is our personal identity, our self, our 'I am', a gift from the I AM who created us. Jesus gently insists we must surrender this 'life' (25) to him, or we will never keep it. He has shown us how (26).

'The principle runs through all life from top to bottom. Give up yourself, and you will find your real self… Submit to death, death of your ambitions and favourite wishes every day… Keep back nothing. Nothing that you have not given away will ever be really yours. Look only for yourself, and you will find in the long run only hatred, loneliness, despair, rage, ruin, and decay. But look for Christ and you will find him, and with him everything else thrown in.' *(C.S. Lewis)*

DAY 57: THE ONLY GOOD MESSIAH . . .

'Jesus Christ is a God we can approach without pride and before whom we can humble ourselves without despair.'

(Pascal)

John 12:27-36

Magazines and radio programmes often tell us about stress: what causes it, the terrible things it leads to, how to avoid it, deal with it, and so on. Did Jesus ever experience stress?

In one sense, no. The records of his life show us someone very much in control of himself — unhurried, unruffled by criticism and opposition. But verse 27 shows, along with passages like Luke 22:42-44, that the man Jesus was deeply apprehensive about the Cross, and was constantly tempted to find a different way to draw people to himself (32; compare with 31, Luke 4:5-7).

Here again, however, he deals with the pressure: to be saved from 'this hour' would be to deny the whole purpose for which he came to the world (23,27).

Doesn't the Messiah live for ever, leading his people to victory, the people ask (34)? Yes and no, Jesus says. In one sense, the only good Messiah is a dead one.

The other gods were strong; but Thou wast weak;
They rode, but Thou didst stumble to a throne,
But to our wounds only God's wounds can speak,
And not a god has wounds, but Thou alone. *(Edward Shillito)*

Jesus, I bring you the wounds that others have inflicted on me, and those I have inflicted on others, for your healing.
Lord, I bring you the stress in my life — help me to separate out the purposeful from the fruitless.

If there is something you want me to do, but I fear to face up to, show me — and hold my hand.

DAY 58: WHAT MAKES THIS RAGE AND SPITE?

My song is love unknown; my Saviour's love to me; love to the loveless shown, that they might lovely be. *(Samuel Crossman)* Lord, keep working on this 'loveless one', please.

John 19:16-24

Who put Jesus on the cross? What had Jesus done that deserved such a death?

Pilate and the Romans? Yes. Though he was convinced of Jesus' innocence (18:38; 19:4,6,12), to pacify the crowd, Pilate weakly handed him over to the Roman soldiers, who nailed him to the cross.
The Leaders of the Jewish people? Yes. It was they who forced Pilate's hand. Why? Out of envy we are told; Jesus was everything they should have been, and were not.
Judas Iscariot? Yes. It was Judas who rejected Jesus' friendship and final appeal, and betrayed him to the Jews.

Behind all of these we can see the evil face of Satan, 'the prince of this world', taking revenge on the one who dared to challenge his rule.

More mysterious yet, these things happened because 'God had already planned and decided that Jesus would be handed over to you.' (Acts 2:23) And the picture is still incomplete: see the next two readings.

If you have time, try to read the whole of chapters 18 and 19 at one sitting in the next day or so.

If you found yourself in any of these situations, do you think you might have acted differently?

Thanks be to you, Lord Jesus Christ,
for all the benefits which you have won for us,
(and) for all the pains and insults which you have borne for us.
Richard of Chichester (13th Century)

We read the second half of this prayer in Reading 22.

DAY 59: SO MUCH LOVE, SO MUCH PAIN

Spend a few minutes in silence. Focus on the word 'love'. What feelings does the word give you? Does it make you feel warm, vulnerable, disappointed, contented, safe? Bring your feelings before God. Be honest with him.

John 19:25-30

Poor Mary. So this was what old Simeon had meant all those years ago when he said 'you, Mary, will suffer as though you had been stabbed by a dagger' (Luke 2:35). But 'with all that love, who could have thought there could be so much pain.' *(Tom Wright)*

Who could have thought it?

Jesus could. Time and again, he had explained to his dull-witted disciples that 'the Son of Man must be killed…'

God could. Hundreds of years before, he had described, through Isaiah, how his servant would be 'despised and rejected', and 'pierced for our sins', and how he would 'pour out his life'. If you have time, read the whole of Isaiah 53 and Psalm 22; reflect on the 'coincidences' between what was written then and what happened when Jesus died.

Now, 'Everything is done!' (30): the great rescue operation, planned and foretold by God, sweated on and suffered for by Jesus, was done, complete.

And while the shouts of the angels echoed round heaven, at the foot of the cross one small human transaction put flesh on the miracle, as Jesus' mother and his friend John accepted each other into a new family, a foretaste of the Kingdom.

Lord, help me to look beyond myself, even though I have some unresolved pain. Assist me this week to go out on a limb and reach out to someone nearby, or even to humbly accept someone else's love or listening ear.

DAY 60: A DEBT WE COULDN'T PAY

Father, your constant love for us is strange and beautiful. And our persistence is amazing too. We ignore you, reject your will for our lives, and stubbornly prefer our ideas to yours. Thankyou that your dealings with us go beyond justice and judgement.

John 19:31-42

On his deathbed, Heinrich Heine casually observed 'God will forgive me, it's his trade.' No, Heinrich. We can't invent a god to suit our need. God's trade is righteousness: forgiveness is his desire — and his problem. His profound problem is the clash of divine perfection and human rebellion. Collision between these is inevitable, because of who God is and who we are. At the point of impact we find the cross of Christ, the place where heaven's love and justice meet.

Here Jesus died. Who caused his death? More than the envy and fear of priests, the actions of Judas and Pilate, more than the justice and judgement of God, it was my sin and yours that put him there. We cannot repay this debt which he chose to pay for us.

In *Pilgrim's Progress*, John Bunyan describes a dream where Christian, loaded up with sin, comes upon a place where a cross stands. Nearby, further down, is a tomb. Suddenly, Christian's burden loosens. It falls from his shoulders, rolls into the open tomb and disappears. Relieved of his great burden, Christian is filled with joy.

This is a picture of what happens to our sin when we recognise and take hold of the meaning of Jesus' death on the Cross. Then we experience relief and exhilaration as our sin disappears for ever and God wipes the slate clean.

Where is your burden? What can you do with it?

DAY 61: AS FIRE BY BURNING

Lord, I live too much of my life behind locked doors of embarrassment, shyness and fear. Come gently into my heart, speak the peace I need to hear, lead me into situations where I can share your peace.

John 20:19-23

Try drawing a 'resurrection truth flow chart' — an ideas map, where the arrows mean 'and therefore…':

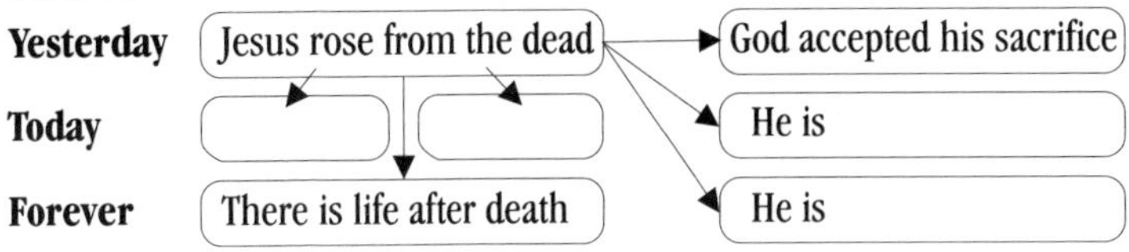

Jesus appeared many times to his disciples (see 1 Corinthians 15:3-8), but this occasion is specially important for the church. One word for 'sending' (21) is 'mission'. Emil Brunner, a theologian, said: 'The church exists by mission as fire by burning.' What do you think he meant? Jesus sends us out as he was sent, to be alongside people, to *be* as well as to *tell* good news from God.

As we go, he gives us:

Peace (21, NIV) — peace with God and the peace of God (the Jewish greeting *Shalom* means peace)

Purpose (21) — meaning and direction for our lives

Power (22) — not only God the Father, over us, and God the Son with us, but God the Spirit, *in* us

Christ has no body now on earth but yours, no hands but yours, no feet but yours; yours are the eyes through which to look with Christ's compassion … yours are the feet with which he is to go about doing good… (*Teresa of Avila*). Is there a situation you are aware of now where Christ has need of your hands, feet or eyes?

DAY 62: WOULD YOU DIE FOR A LIE?

Do these thoughts apply to you?
My faith isn't always strong
Sometimes I doubt whether I am a real Christian.
Sometimes I wonder whether God is there at all.
I wish I could be absolutely certain in my beliefs.

John 20:24-31

We all have doubts. Nothing that matters can be proved beyond doubt. Thomas shows us how to cope:
❍ Admit your doubts (25) — to yourself, to God, to close fellow-Christians. If doubts are taboo in a Christian group, remember this makes it a brittle, dangerous place. ❍ Obey what you *are* sure of (28). Obedience and faith are entwined and hard to separate. ❍ If faith is hard, how about unbelief? Can you be sure that the world came about just by chance and that Jesus is dead for ever? Does this demand an even greater leap of 'faith'? For myself, I find it 'difficult to believe, but impossible not to!'

Consider these eleven peasants and fishermen who:
❍ all abandoned their leader at his time of need ❍ were left terrified and in hiding after the seemingly horrible fiasco of his death as a criminal
❍ between them had little or no education or status
Yet, unknown to them, they were about to go out and start the most influential religion in history. Nearly all would die refusing to deny their faith in Jesus.

The scholar C.F.D. Moule says that the birth and rise of the Christian church, 'rips a great hole in history, a hole the size and shape of the resurrection'. If you refuse the church's explanation, he asks, with what will you fill the hole?

'I do have faith! Please help me to have even more' (Mark 9:24).

THE GOD WHO LEADS HIS PEOPLE

INTRODUCTION TO READINGS 63 TO 70, IN THE PSALMS, THE PROPHET EZEKIEL, AND JOHN'S GOSPEL.

In his book, *Knowing God*, J.I. Packer says 'The Bible puts flesh on ... bare bones of ideas by using pictures and analogies, telling us that we know God in the manner of a son knowing his father, a wife knowing her husband, a subject knowing his king, and a sheep knowing its shepherd.' God reveals himself in ways our tiny minds can grasp.

We'll be looking at God as Shepherd, and ourselves as sheep. Middle-Eastern shepherds worked in very different ways to modern sheep farmers:

- Sheep were kept mainly for wool. The shepherd got to know them, and they him. (Even today in the Middle-East, mixed-up flocks can be separated out simply by the calls of their shepherds.)
- There were no fences or walls, and often little grass, so sheep would wander far.
- Wolves and thieves were a constant threat.
- Because of the dangers, the shepherd walked ahead of his flock.

An Arab tour guide was explaining the background to this story to a party of tourists. Just as he finished describing how shepherds managed their sheep, through the bus windows the tourists saw a man driving a flock of sheep along with a stick. Tearing off to investigate, the guide came back with a big smile: 'Ladies and gentlemen, he is not the shepherd. He is in fact the butcher!'

In the previous section the focus was especially on God's holiness, on how totally different he is from us. In this section we'll see more of his nearness, his love, and his warm, detailed, personal care for us. Somehow we'll have to learn to hold both these truths together!

DAY 63: GOD IS ALL I NEED

God is a generous giver. Write down some of his most precious gifts to you — material, emotional, spiritual, eternal. Ask yourself then, which means more to you, the gifts or the Giver?

Psalm 23

David trusted God to be his Provider and his Protector. Can you think of ways God has provided for and protected you? Looking at this psalm from another angle, can you expect God's provision and protection if you are not prepared to follow and obey him?

The idea of handing over the right to make our own decisions is very hard for individualistic 'modern' people, including Christians. Have you ever tried to explain to someone why you are trying to live each day according to another person's agenda, and God's agenda at that? They probably suggested you were 'off the planet'! But David is glad that 'Your shepherd's rod and staff protect me' (GNB). His shepherd has both a club to defend the sheep, and a long crook to guide the sheep, if necessary, with a whack on the back!

A modern version of the psalm begins:
The Lord my shepherd rules my life
and gives me all I need. *(Christopher Idle)*

Can you learn to trust God more? Take what's on your mind — decisions to make, needs to meet — and hand them over to your Shepherd.

Over the next day or so, meditate on the first five words of the psalm:

YOU, Lord... the only one, unique, pre eminent...

You, LORD... have the right to run my life...

You, Lord, ARE...

You, Lord, are MY...

You, Lord, are my SHEPHERD...

DAY 64: OUR ONLY HOPE

The most basic prayer of all is “Help!” When we feel comfortable and in charge of our lives, prayer can become polite and distant, a one way conversation touching only the fringes of our lives. But when we’re desperate, prayer is nothing less than life or death.

Psalm 80

Perhaps this psalm was written during the Assyrian invasion described in 2 Kings 18:9-12. We don’t know, but the circumstances were serious. Instead of the firm, gentle provider and protector of Psalm 23, God is now the accuser and judge. Yet God’s people turn to him — they have no-one else.

As he went to one of Hitler’s gas chambers, a Jew scribbled this prayer: ‘God you have disregarded my pleadings. You have failed your own people. You have been heartless, cruel and deaf beyond belief...You have done your worst. But I will not let you go!’

About 40 per cent of Israel’s songs (the Psalms) show attitudes of turning to God in discouragement or questioning. Few contemporary Christian songs express this ‘we’re-in-trouble-you’re-our-only-hope’ feeling. Are we too comfortable these days?

In a second contrast with Psalm 23, the Lord is not ‘my’ but ‘our’ shepherd, the shepherd of God’s covenant people Israel. Is God a shepherd to people today? Some would place their nation or present-day Israel into that slot but the church probably fits best.

The church is under various kinds of attack today, from opposition outside or from false teaching, doubt and complacency within. Many churches could well pray: ‘Lord God All-Powerful, make us strong again!’(19)

Are the prayers of your church or small group too casual? Dull? Or are they rainbows of praise, adoration and desperate need? Ask God to bring them to life.

DAY 65: POWER CORRUPTS...

Lord, speak to me, that I may speak
In living echoes of Thy tone
As Thou hast sought, so let me seek
Thy erring children, lost and lone. *(Frances Ridley Havergal)*

Ezekiel 34:1-10

God has always appointed 'under-shepherds' to care for his people. The work is described in the New Testament as 'worthwhile' (1 Timothy 3:1); a privilege in other words.
Israel's shepherds (all their leaders — kings, priests, generals, judges) certainly seem to have got this part of the message: they had seized their privileges with both hands (2,3).
But 'power corrupts…'. Corruption begins when we blur the knowledge that God holds each of us accountable for the way we carry out any work he gives us. It applies today, as much as in those days.
Locked in with the *privileges* of leadership are the *responsibilities*, illustrated in verses 2-6, and the *dangers*, revealed in 7-10.
'Much is required', Jesus said, 'of those to whom much is given.' (Luke 12:48, Living Bible)

We need to take these principles seriously in at least two areas:
Ourselves — we all have some leadership role, some capacity to encourage or discourage others in their walk with God.
Reflect on the privileges and responsibilities you have. Have you neglected a part of your responsibility or overlooked someone who needs your companionship and encouragement?
Our leaders — consider the burdens taken on by the leader(s) of your church. Give them all the respect and encouragement you can. However, don't be afraid to bring matters to their attention tactfully when they appear to be distracted by other concerns. Above all, never imagine that they are too holy to need your prayers!

DAY 66: COME TO ME

'When he saw the crowds, he felt sorry for them. They were confused and helpless, like sheep without a shepherd.' (Matthew 9:36) Who comes to mind? Bring them forward one by one, sharing your concerns for them with Jesus.

Ezekiel 34:11-16

While in exile in Babylon, Ezekiel heard from God. He had a depressing message to tell his fellow-exiles, that Jerusalem was soon be destroyed and most of the people in their homeland were to be killed or taken into captivity (see chapters 1 to 24).

In our last reading we saw how this judgement became necessary partly because of the failure of the leaders of the nation. Today, God reveals how full of compassion he is for the innocent sheep betrayed and badly treated by their leaders.

The passage is full of promises. How many can you find? Who makes them? Who do they apply to?

In one of these promises (15) God says that he himself will be the shepherd of his people. Yet soon after (23) he seems to promise a human shepherd. If this seems too hard to puzzle out, wait till you get to Reading 68.

Today, sadly, in the flocks of God's people there are many who have been wounded or disappointed by the failure of a Christian leader. Some of these wounded are no longer within the flock or feel they can never join it: hypocrisy, pride, greed, dishonesty, immorality and many other forms of lovelessness have all played their part in their leaving or not entering. You probably know one or more of them. Now too, you also know how God feels about these hurting people. Bring them to him in prayer. What can you do to care for them?

DAY 67: TAKING SIDES

Living in an affluent country, can you think of ways our society directly or indirectly adds to the suffering of those less well off? From what you have learned of God's character, does God lean more towards the rich or the poor?

Ezekiel 34:17-31

As Thucydides said, around 400 BC — 'the powerful exact what they can and the weak grant what they must'. Millions around the world know exactly what he means, as they endure awful injustices from corrupt officials, violent husbands or playground bullies. They can only grind their teeth and scream in helpless rage.

God is not 'Sovereign Lord' for nothing: he *will* judge between the strong and the weak (20). Those whose pasture has been muddied (18) or who have been butted off the good pasture (21) can trust that he *will* even the scales of justice — in his time, not ours (Romans 12:19-21).

Many of us are more like 'the fat and the strong' (16), the 'strong sheep' (20) — accountable to God. 'Much is required...' applies to us too. If we love God, we will also want to be on his side, using our power to seek justice for the weak *now*: 'See that justice is done ... help those in need' (Isaiah 1:17).

The last section (23-31) describes the renewal of God's covenant under the Messiah, the Son of David, and the rich blessings that spill over, now and eternally, to his people.

'...a church that does not exist to take the side of the poor, to denounce injustice and to hold up righteousness, is a church that has no right to be...' *(the great Baptist preacher Charles Spurgeon)*. How do you and your church rate?

DAY 68: HE KNOWS MY NAME!

'The perfect friend is one who knows the worst about you,
And loves you just the same...' *(Anon.)*
Do you have friends like this? Thank God for them.

John 10:1-6

Just before this reading comes the story of Jesus' healing of a man born blind. The Jewish leaders reacted critically to this, showing how blind and spiteful they were. Jesus uses these shepherd pictures to try to show them how off-course they are, and to teach his own followers to discern a true leader from a false one.

One thing that comes out is that Jesus' leadership is based not on rules but on relationship:

He calls his sheep 'by name'(3). Tom Skinner, who had proved his toughness by becoming leader of a New York gang, met Jesus. Writing in *Black and Free* he said: 'For the first time in my life I have *dignity*. I don't have to fight for it. I *am*, present tense, a son of God. I don't have to break my neck to prove it. I don't have to fight to be recognized. I have already been recognized by the Lord of heaven and earth as his son.'

His sheep 'follow, because they know his voice' (4). It takes practice to learn to recognise this voice. It may speak through the encouragement or example of godly leaders or friends, through sermons or songs as you worship, through the voice of your conscience, or in other ways, but most often he will use his written word.

What matters most in life is not that we are able to know God, but that God chooses to *know us*. What does this knowledge do for you?

DAY 69: LIFE, MORE AND BETTER

'All off us were like sheep that had wandered off. We had each gone our own way' (Isaiah 53:6).
Ask God to show you these 'ways'.

John 10:7-10

Many Eastern houses had a sheep pen built alongside. The shepherd slept across its entrance, becoming a human gate — a barrier to thieves, a way in for the sheep (7,9). With the shepherd to lead them out to pasture and in to safety, the sheep had everything necessary for life (10). How sad to be a sheep without a shepherd: no wonder Jesus' heart went out to people like this (Matthew 9:36).

In Patricia St John's lovely children's story, *The Tanglewoods' Secret* (Scripture Union), Ruth, a rebellious and unhappy 9-year-old, runs away from home and shelters in the village church. Next morning, the kindly minister finds her and takes her to his home. She notices a picture of 'a sheep lost on a mountainside… the sheep looks up and cries to be rescued; someone has heard… the shepherd is leaning over the precipice…'. While talking about the lost lamb, the girl realises the minister is now talking about her. '…you are still trying to get back without Him', he explains, '…You tell me you try to be good, but you keep being naughty instead… What you've got to do is to stop trying to make yourself good; you've got to tell the Shepherd that you are quite lost, and ask Him to find you, and make you one of His own obedient lambs.' 'Will He really?' Ruth asks. 'He's been loving you and looking for you for nine years', he answers.

If you need the Good Shepherd's assistance why keep trying to solve things alone?

DAY 70: THE UNDER-SHEPHERD'S PATTERN

The *good* Shepherd: this is not the usual word the original Greek of the New Testament uses for 'good', but another, *kalos*. My little dictionary says this means 'beautiful, as an outward sign of the inward good, noble, honourable character'. Take a little time to wonder at this more-than-skin-deep beauty. Dare to pray the words of the old hymn, 'May the beauty of Jesus be seen in me...'

John 10:11-21

What does this Shepherd do for his sheep that shows his goodness and earns him their love?

He serves them (11) — in his living as much as his dying, he lays down his life.

He guards them (12)

He knows them (14) — and makes himself known.

He seeks them (16)

And, as we have seen earlier, **he leads them** (3,4) and **feeds them** (9).

Peter tells the elders of the churches, 'Just as shepherds watch over their sheep, you must watch over everyone God has placed in your care.' (1 Peter 5:1-4) In contrast to the selfish and power-hungry leaders we thought about in Readings 65 to 68, Christian leaders have no choice but to model themselves on The Shepherd.

The New Testament often tells us to 'care for', 'serve', 'encourage', 'build up', 'teach' one another. We are all under-shepherds in some sense.

The reading asks us to face *up* and *out*:

❍ Don't leave today's reading without squarely facing the Lord Jesus. Thank him for all he has done for you, even though you are sometimes a tiresome and obstinate sheep!

❍ Turn round, and with his hand on your shoulder, look outwards to the shepherdless sheep all around you. To which ones is he sending you?

Check point H

GOD CHAMPIONS THE OPPRESSED

INTRODUCTION TO READINGS 71 TO 77, IN LUKE'S GOSPEL, PSALMS AND ISAIAH.

God's desire for all people can be summed up as *Shalom*: peace + prosperity + harmony + justice (see Reading 53). The absence of these is 'poverty'. The Bible does not draw too hard a line between spiritual, emotional and material poverty, but it does treat it as something we should neither accept with a shrug of the shoulders — 'it's God's will' — nor blame for its victims — 'they're so lazy'. Rather, it teaches that a large part of the cause of poverty lies in the greed and indifference of the powerful.

We begin with vivid and treasured memories of Mary the mother of Jesus. It is not surprising that it is from a woman, and from Mary in particular, that we get deep insights into Jesus' revolutionary attitudes towards the powerful and the weak in this world.

The lessons of the Old Testament cannot all be applied directly to the church (because it is not a political body, as was Israel), or to any particular nation (because it is not 'God's people', as was Israel). But since its message reflects the nature of God, it can and should challenge both church and nation. 'The church… is not the master or the servant of the state, but rather the conscience of the state.' *(Martin Luther King)*

When Isaiah was writing during the 8th century BC, it was for Israel a time of great prosperity and religious enthusiasm, alongside growing moral and social disorder. Over the centuries, Christians have failed to learn the lesson that while times of persecution can be hard, times of prosperity are far more dangerous to faith, both for individuals and for the church.

The right gear

With the help of Foothold you have begun your adventure with the Bible... and with God.

Now let Scripture Union's other resources help you to keep going.

Scripture Union has for over 100 years been providing meditation resources to help people grow with the Bible.

On many occasions in the Bible, God's word is described as bread, milk, meat - food for the Christian's journey through life.

After you have completed this book in the *Foothold* series, take some decisions to firm up your faith. Equip yourself on a regular basis for faithful Christian living. Aim to find day-by-day nourishment for your life.

Order the other two books in the *Foothold* series or check out the quarterly Bible guides published by Scripture Union. They're available for you and for people of all ages (including children and young people). They're for people new to regular Bible reading and experienced Christians alike.

Use the coupon below to put yourself in touch with these resources. There are more details on the next page. Cut out the coupon and send it to your nearest Scripture Union office. The address is on page 126.

Dear Scripture Union,

I am interested to know more about Scripture Union's Bible resources. Please supply the information as indicated on the reverse of this reply coupon.

My name ______________________

Address ______________________

Postcode ______________________

Scripture Union's Bible resources... for a firm foothold on faith

Foothold
The other two books in the series will give you a firmer grip on the Bible's message and help you find a *Foothold* for your faith. Each book has another 100 specially selected Bible readings. *Understanding the Bible* will give you a quick overview of what the Bible is really about. You will explore the central message of the most popular book of all time. The stories and themes will begin to hang together and you will feel more confident about your faith. *Knowing Ourselves* will give you insights about how God sees the great variety of human beings he created. We discover his dreams for people alongside their stumbles and failings. We begin to see ourselves - our strengths and weaknesses through the eyes of the characters and teachings of the Bible. A different perspective altogether!

Daily Bread
Scripture Union's best seller! A quarterly book for adults with devotional readings for every day. The comments from an international team of writers are direct, practical and zesty. Also available in large print format. Includes outlines for group discussion and a variety of features.

Encounter with God
A thought provoking Bible reading quarterly for people who like to be stretched. Ideal for experienced Bible readers.

Alive to God
A quarterly framework for regular time with God. A fresh and creative approach to God's word for adults. Guided prayer, worship, reflection, action.

Something for everyone
There are Scripture Union resources for all age groups from pre-schoolers to adults.

Dear Scripture Union,
Please send

- ❑ a sample copy of Daily Bread and a full catalogue of Scripture Union Bible resources.
- ❑ information about becoming a local church representative to promote Bible reading in my congregation.

Remember to print you name and address on the front of this reply coupon and send to your nearest office of Scripture Union. The address is on page 126 of this book.

DAY 71: NO ORDINARY BIRTH

Think of some people you value and respect — and one or two for whom you have little time. On what basis did you rate them? How might God's estimation of them compare with yours?

Luke 1:26-38

An event foretold thousands of years before is about to take place. It is to be a watershed in history; the world's calendar will be reset around it. The creator of people everywhere is about to become a person himself. All the heavenly beings are watching and waiting — and it all hangs upon the response of a 14-year-old village girl. What a story!

Luke, the medical doctor and careful historian, knew as well as Mary did, that babies needed fathers for conception — normally (34). He presents the story as historical truth: 'The Holy Spirit will come down to you and God's power will come over you. So your child will be called the holy Son of God.' Why should we, as some people do, make this a barrier to belief? After all, 'From God's point of view there are no miracles.' *(St Augustine)*

Jesus was to undertake a dangerous journey, culminating in a head-on challenge to the power structures of his day. How right that he should begin this journey not only by being born a helpless baby, but born of an ordinary young girl, unknown to anyone of importance. And how beautiful is Gabriel's affirmation of her (28). Truly, God 'chose the weak things of this world to put the powerful to shame.' (1 Corinthians 1:27)

The whole prospect of motherhood in these circumstances must have been frightening to young Mary. Do you find it difficult to agree willingly to God's way in your life (38)?

DAY 72: REJOICE WITH THOSE WHO REJOICE

William Tyndale, the 16th century Bible translator wrote that the truth of the gospel made him feel so 'good, merry, glad and joyful' that he was compelled to 'sing, dance, and leap for joy' and to 'laugh from the low bottom of his heart.' Have you experienced times of joy since you have got to know God? How do you express your feelings?

Luke 1:39-45

Mary's relative Elizabeth also had good reasons for joy. Not only was a longed-for child on the way (and a *boy*!) but the promise of his birth was announced by an angel who said he was intended for greatness (1:12-17). Elizabeth could well have been put out by this girl (young enough to be her granddaughter) who arrived unexpectedly, upstaging her story with an even better one. Great privileges had been given to Elizabeth and she could easily have become proud and resented Mary. But filled with the Spirit, and open to God, she responds to Mary with genuine joy and wholehearted encouragement.

Do you have a particular responsibility in your work or church? When another person displays greater gifts than you in this area, how do you feel? Do you gain pleasure from seeing them fail, or criticise them behind their backs?

Can you think of any in your church who are more gifted than you in areas where you have ability (sport, cooking, singing, leadership, looking good, Christian service, etc.) Think how much God loves them. Pray that he will bless them and use their gifts richly. Know he loves you too and wants to use your gifts, as well as develop new ones in you.

DAY 73: THE GREAT REVERSAL

The Swiss writer and psychiatrist Paul Tournier wrote sadly about the sickness of 'our headlong dash for power'. Mentioning all kinds of power: military, political, economic and the power of propaganda, technology, sexual desires, muscular strength and money, he reflects that, 'The glorification of the powerful has gone along with the devaluation of the weak, the old, the sensitive, the shy, the scrupulous, the odd, the abandoned and the dreamers.' Mary appears to identify with his observations.

Luke 1:46-56

Mary's heart brims over with thankfulness for what God has done for her. Her mind is so in tune with Scripture that she refers to over eight Old Testament passages. To her, what God has done is totally in keeping with what he *is* — and what he will do. So here she worships him.

Oppression takes many forms — the company that exploits its workers, the adult who abuses a child, the official who takes bribes, the government that represses a minority… One thing all oppressors have in common, is that to them, the people they oppress are unimportant — they are only peasants, only children, etc. They don't matter. But one thing that comes through strongly in this song is that to God the humble and the hungry *do* matter.

Who of your friends are among the humble and hungry or suffering in other less visible ways? Pray for them now. If you are unaware of anyone close to you who needs your prayers, then something is missing in your life. Ask God to make you more mindful of the needs of others. For starters, is there something you could do with someone who is needy — materially, emotionally or spiritually (*with* them, not just *for* them).

DAY 74: A FRESH START

Jesus, shine in my darkness like the rising of the sun;
rescue me from my enemies,
help me to serve you without fear,
and guide my feet into the path of peace.

Luke 1:57-80

Zechariah describes events still to happen as if they have already occurred. English does not convey accurately the original sense of 'God … has come' (68, compare 51-54). Zechariah considers these events already done, precisely because God has promised them! 'You, my son' refers to John the Baptist, and 'the Lord' is the Messiah, Jesus. John's role will be to 'go ahead of the Lord to get things ready for him'(76).

Mary has just described a future revolution , where the relationships between the rulers/rich and the humble/hungry they live off will be put right. But before things can be put right between people, things must be put right between them and God. The sin which comes between them must be repented of and removed. This is the great rescue and reconciliation that Zechariah talks about: first a reconciliation (77) between us and God and then our rescue (68,71,74) from the forces of evil, into whose hands we fall whenever we back away from God.

For the oppressed, this should be the beginning of a new self-respect and courage. Remember Tom Skinner's 'I have *dignity*' in Reading 68? For the oppressor, or even the oppressor's friend, there is the beginning of a new ability to see people as God sees them.

Do you have real enemies? Who or what prevents you becoming the person God meant you to be? Is the hindrance outside you, or inside? Ask God for that reconciliation/rescue package that Zechariah talks about here. No one is excluded from a fresh start.

DAY 75: HALLELUJAH! THIS IS OUR GOD!

Beauty for brokenness, hope for despair,
Lord in your suffering world this is our prayer.
Bread for the children, justice, joy, peace,
Sunrise to sunset your kingdom increase. *(Graham Kendrick)*

Psalm 146

'Praise the Lord!' Yes, for sure, but for what, exactly? Unless we spell this out from time to time, the phrase can become an empty slogan. Check through the psalm; pick out what it tells you about God. What stands out most to you at this moment?

Sometimes a truth in Scripture will come home to a person with added force and relevance, because of their particular situation. What special importance might this psalm have to a Christian:

❍ unjustly imprisoned by a corrupt regime?
❍ serving in the parliament of their nation? (read Exodus 22:21-24)
❍ living in comfort in a wealthy suburb?

Does the fact that *God* promises to look after the needy mean *we* don't need to bother about them?

In Matthew 6:33, Jesus promises that if we put God first, he will look after our needs. But beware of the trap in this statement. It does *not* reduce our responsibility to share what we have; in fact it strengthens the idea. God's most common way of serving the poor is through the caring acts of others.

Can you think of people in each of the categories in verses 7-9? Pray for them.

If you don't know any people like these, why not get in touch with one of the organisations that works with them, either overseas or in your own country. Find out how you can help.

DAY 76: HAVE BLOOD, WILL BOIL[1]

For Christians, prayer is not supposed to be a weapon for battering God —getting our will done in heaven. Rather, it is a way of getting God's will done on earth. Run your mind over the last news bulletin you heard, over the families in your neighbourhood. Is God's will being done?

Isaiah 1:10-20

Things were good for the wealthy in Judah around 750 BC. They had their businesses and pleasant homes — that was life; they made their prayers and sacrifices in the temple — that was religion. Was there a connection between religion and life? Yes, of course, 'my sacrifices must be doing the job — look how prosperous I am!'

But God found their worship worthless (13-15) since their behaviour denied his character. They had forgotten that our God makes moral demands. Then Isaiah reminded them: Sodom and Gomorrah (10) were cities destroyed by God for their immorality (and their greed — see Ezekiel 16:48-50). Billy Graham has said 'If God does not judge our western society, he will have to apologise to Sodom and Gomorrah'.

We too are in deep trouble but God doesn't give up. He offers us the same choice as Judah — 'willingly obey' or 'turn against me'(19,20).

Not all in Judah were guilty of oppressing the poor; but God's people are called to do more than be harmless citizens. He wants us to actively seek justice, to be righteously indignant on behalf of the powerless (17). 'We will have to repent in this generation not merely for the vitriolic words and actions of the bad people, but for the appalling silence of the good people' *(Martin Luther King)*. What are you and your church doing?

[1] 'Have Blood, Will Boil' is from an album by the group *Hunters and Collectors*.

DAY 77: BE DOERS OF THE WORD

'Let my heart be broken by the things that break the heart of God.' *(Bob Pierce, founder of World Vision)*

Isaiah 1:21-31

Isaiah uses several images to bring Judah's rebellion into focus — the wife who has become a prostitute (21), the silver become impure, the wine diluted (22). Each picture describes something good which has gone bad. Each one drives home the message that, however much religion is added to it, a self-centred life is both belittling for those involved and an affront and a deep sadness to God.

He accuses them of getting into Canaanite fertility worship (29). Perhaps this was actually happening. Or was God saying that to worship him with no concern for justice was as bad as worshipping a pagan god — that is a god with no moral character.

The people have become, in effect, murderers (21). In our world, where 30 children die every minute from preventable and poverty-related causes, do we need to ask ourselves, 'How much is my indifference contributing to this?'

It may be that, over the next generation or so, wealthy, powerful, 'Christian' western society will be shown to be like the great oak of verse 30, or the mighty man of verse 31. Mercifully, God's judgements are never just aimless revenge; they are designed to purify and restore (25-27).

Look back over the readings in this section. Has God been saying anything to you? 'The one thing that matters is that we always say Yes to God whenever we experience him'

(Lady Julian of Norwich).

This is hard. Pray for someone to stand beside you in being a 'doer' of God's word.

THE GOD WHO ALWAYS LOVES

INTRODUCTION TO READINGS 78 TO 89, IN HOSEA, ROMANS, 1 JOHN AND PSALMS.

Talking to a group of students, a speaker asked what significant facts they knew about Hitler. Gradually the whole catalogue poured out: aggression, violence, hatred, the holocaust, defeat, suicide … not one good thing. 'You've missed the most important', he said. His audience was beaten. 'The most important thing about Hitler was that God loved him.' Silence.

Hosea, a prophet in the dying years of the northern kingdom Israel, was called by God to a costly acting out of a message to his people. To fill out the 8th century BC background, read 2 Kings chapters 14 to 20.

Paul's letter to the Romans is a wonderfully detailed explanation of the Gospel. Through it shines the presence of a God who *wants* to be reconciled to his people, a God who is on our side.

The letter, 1 John, was probably written by John the Gospel writer, about 90 AD, in a time of doubt and confusion. John wrote to assure his 'beloved children' that they could be *sure* that they knew God and had life (5:12,13).

Beware. This God who is Love is what he is, not necessarily what we imagine him or even want him to be. 'An impersonal God — well and good. A subjective God of beauty, truth and goodness, inside our own heads, better still. A formless life force surging through us, a vast power which we can tap, best of all. But God himself, alive, pulling at the other end of the string… that is quite another matter.' *(C.S. Lewis, 'Miracles')*

We end with a psalm, a lyrical celebration of God.

DAY 78: GOD – A LOVING HUSBAND

A list of members of a jury in 17th century England includes 'More Fruit Fowler', 'Kill Sin Roberts', and 'Fight the Good Fight White'. Clearly the godly and much maligned Puritans believed in giving meaningful names! If similar customs were popular today, what name might you take to express the driving principle of your life?

Hosea 1

The people of Israel in Hosea's time found the cult of Baal more attractive than ever. This cult pictured Baal as a husband, who fertilised the land and its people. 'Worship' consisted largely of sexual orgies with male and female cult prostitutes. It is amazing that in the context of local Canaanite society where sex was debased in this way, God took this husband-wife model, stripped and cleansed it from its fertility-cult connections, and then used it to picture his own relationship with his people Israel.

'Marry', he says to Hosea (2). Bible commentators nearly all agree that the description 'an adulterous wife' probably looks into the future. Gomer, like Israel in the days when she was at least relatively faithful to God, begins by being a good wife.

Three children are born, and all are given names that invite questions — with answers that people will not like: Jezreel, 'God scatters' (4), Lo-Ruhamah, 'No Mercy' (6), meaning the end of God's mercy to Israel, and Lo-Ammi, 'Not My People' (9), the end of his relationship with them.

When God's oversees our life he may lead us, like Hosea, into experiences which bring grief we cannot understand at the time. God knows what he is doing; in his will, nothing is without meaning or purpose. Trust him now for anything that you, your family, or friends are going through.

DAY 79: A DANGEROUS GOD TO BELONG TO

Relationships always have two sides.
Give some examples in the gaps below.

Being a	Privileges	Obligations
Student or employee	________________	________________
Wife or husband	________________	________________
Child of God	________________	________________

Hosea 2:2-13

It has happened. Gomer has gone to her lovers (5). As Hosea turns this over in his mind and shares with God all his pain and anger, God says to him, 'Do you understand now? This is how *I* feel about Israel, when she leaves me to follow fake religions'. So the passion and the poem that pours out of Hosea includes both Gomer *and* Israel.

Why did Gomer go? Why was Israel unfaithful? Apparently her lovers promised more of the 'good things of life' (5). False religions are too varied to sum up in one line. Like the Baal cults, most of them offer their pleasures (such as material goods or sensual experiences) immediately. The accounts are sent later.

What neither Gomer nor Israel could see, and so often ourselves, is that the good things we enjoy come from God (8).

The normal response of a cheated husband in Bible times was to divorce, humiliate and punish the unfaithful wife (2,3, 9-13), because of failure to keep her part of the agreement.

Almighty God offers us an intimate relationship, and takes the appalling risk of allowing us, if we so wish, to step away from it. What does it do to God when we do so? What does it do to us? When did you last do this to God? Quietly meditate on what you might do about this.

DAY 80: GRIEF BECOMES GOSPEL

'The greatest thing in all my life is knowing You... loving You serving You... I want to know You more... love You more... serve You more.' *(Mark Pendergrass)*

Some people feel uncomfortable singing songs to God that seem more like human love-songs. Is this because our human love is shot through with impurity? Today's reading shows that, because God's love is so pure and self-giving, Scripture has no problem describing *his* love for *us* in these terms. Now *that* is awe-inspiring!

Hosea 2:14 — 3:5

'I will allure her... court her... woo her... win her back with words of love', are different translations of 2:14. We should be pleading with God, begging to be restored. But wonder of wonders, God is prepared to plead with us.

The last reading was about punishment; now we see the purpose behind it. 'If He puts thorns in your bed, it is only to awaken you from the sleep of spiritual death...' (Whitfield). Often the punishment takes the form of allowing our selfishness to bear its bitter fruit (see Romans 1:24,26,28): Gomer's wilful unfaithfulness leads her in the end to slavery (3:2). Hosea goes the second mile, finds her, redeems her (buys her back). Through how many light years did Jesus come to find *us*? How much did he pay to buy *us* back? (1 Peter 1:18,19)

'To Him I belong by purchase, conquest and self-surrender. To me He belongs for all my daily need.' *(Bishop J. Handley Moule)* Turn this into a prayer: replace 'Him' with 'You'.

DAY 81: INEXHAUSTIBLE LOVE

Think about a time when you helped a person who never thanked you for your assistance? How did you feel?

Hosea 11:1-11

God speaks now (1-4) not as a husband but as a father — one who has loved Israel and chosen (adopted?) her, brought her up, taught her to walk. Think of the hard work parents put in to teach their children to become trusting, forgiving, obedient and hard-working. Think of the hard work God has put in to give his people the laws and experiences which teach them that he is a powerful, trustworthy, moral, holy God.

Israel responded (5-7) with more than simple ingratitude. She deliberately chose things that brought pain to God. It was plain rebellion. God faces an agonising dilemma (8,9): if he is 'the Holy God' (9) and nothing more, then he will give up on Israel, and destroy her; if he is a God who doesn't care, he will look the other way. But he *is* God and not human. Our next readings show how this dilemma is resolved.

Few Old Testament pictures have been developed so richly in the New Testament as the idea of becoming and being a child of God (for example, John 1:11-13; Galatians 4:4-7). The God of all adopts us into his family, with the privileges of being his children and heirs to everything. What a stunning and romantic story. The first chapters begin with God's choosing of the people of Israel. When we know this kind of love we can no longer be the same people. We are touched by grace and become people of destiny. We feel a debt of gratitude. Think about it!

DAY 82: THIS HAPPY CERTAINTY

'To pray is to change. This is a great grace. How good of God to provide a path whereby our lives can be taken over by love and joy and peace and patience ...' *(Richard Foster)* Pray that the truthstream of this reading will flow into the bloodstream of your character, repairing the sin-damaged image of God, healing and empowering you.

Romans 5:1-5

Set in the pure gold of this passage are eight key gospel words, sharp and sparkling.

Justified: God accepts us just as we are, *'Just*-as-*if-I'd-never-sinned'* (read 3:21-26).

Peace: no longer fighting God, having accepted his offer, we now live in tune with God.

Access: we can discuss anything with God at any time; nothing is taboo.

Grace: God totally accepts us; our relationship does not depend on our erratic attempts to please him.

Hope: we can confidently expect to be in God's presence one day, complete, whole, accepted and ready to share whatever good things he has so carefully prepared for us.

Joy: 'Joy is peace dancing, peace is joy resting.' *(Charles Spurgeon)*
With the hope that we now have, no experience, however bitter, need be meaningless or useless. 'He who has a why to live can bear with almost any how.' *(Nietzsche)*

Character: (4) in the original language this word describes how metal is tested and refined by fire (GNB, 'God's approval'). Our time on earth is a similar preparation for our future life with God. Becoming Christ-like doesn't come cheap.

Love: the presence of the Spirit will become obvious in our inner being.

Pray these concepts into your whole life — from your head, to your heart, to your hands. Focus on one for the next 24 hours.

DAY 83: MUCH MORE THAN FIRE INSURANC

Our egos will do anything to be stroked, fed and flattered. Even when dealing with God, we look desperately for some way to believe that *we* contributed something towards our salvation. Even if God did do it all for us, then surely we deserved it … just a bit?

Romans 5:6-11

Why was it necessary for Christ to die for people, ourselves included? What reasons can you find here for this? This reading highlights the self-centred hopes of human religion. The Bible teaches that God loved us because he is love, not because we were lovable. This does nothing for our pride, but at least it is sure. If we had to depend on being good enough, religious enough (clever, beautiful, or anything else) to be accepted by God, how would we ever be sure of scoring a pass mark?

Here we see something of the way God resolved his great dilemma (remember Reading 81?) — how could he reconcile himself to those he made and loved, who then chose to turn away. His justice was only satisfied by the voluntary death of his Son (6). Now he is able to offer his love freely to all (8). Our contribution? Only to accept or to reject this sacrifice and love.

When we accept this wonderful offer, then and only then can we begin to enjoy what it means to be worth so much to God. And the offers lasts! When we face the heat of God's anger against all evil, we can be sure we'll be safe (9,10). Being saved is much more than fire insurance.

Starting from the truths in this reading, work out, then offer to God a 'sorry' prayer, a 'thankyou' prayer, and a 'please' prayer.

DAY 84: GOD IS ON OUR SIDE

In heavenly love abiding, no change my heart shall fear; and safe is such confiding, for nothing changes here. The storm may roar without me, my heart may low be laid, but God is round about me, and can I be dismayed? *(Anna Laetitia Waring)*

Think back to the last 'storm' you were in. How real is it to you that God is round about you?

Romans 8:31-39

Paul seems to be answering an imaginary questioner: 'This gospel of yours is great, Paul, but down here at ground level it's different, you know… things are really against us: all around there are hostile people and menacing spiritual forces; and God is so holy that we can't even feel safe with him.' Do you feel this way at times, too? In response, Paul reels off a volley of unanswerable questions. What is there to fear?

God himself, or Christ? (31-34) But God is on *our* side! Christ? He died for us!

Pressures? (35-37) 'These are the trials through which we triumph.' (Jerusalem Bible)

Cosmic powers? (38,39) 'Powers above or powers below' refer to the positions of stars and planets. How many people do you know who not only read but *believe* their horoscopes? 'Nothing … can ever come between us and the love of God made visible in Christ Jesus our Lord.' (Jerusalem Bible)

'It doesn't matter, really, how great the pressure is; it only matters where the pressure lies. See that it never comes between you and the Lord — then, the greater the pressure the more it presses you to his breast.' *(Hudson Taylor)*

What pressures are on you now? Where are they driving you? Towards God or away from him?

DAY 85: REAL LOVE

I overheard a student, sounding off to friends at lunchtime. She was 'spitting chips'. She had just come from a Scripture class where some arrogant *twit* had claimed that Christians were the only ones who knew about love! What would you have said to her?

1 John 4:7-12

Many people experience deep and wonderful love in the areas of friendship, family, and romance. But all these loves too often have a self-centred element ('I need to have someone to love' — a 'need-love', as C.S. Lewis calls it). Only God's love is pure 'gift-love'.

Yet can *we* know pure love? This kind of love comes only from God. 'Real love isn't our love for God, but his love for us' (10). If it shows up in us, it is evidence of his touch: 'When we love each other, it shows that we have been given new life' (7).

And it shows something else. 'No one has ever seen God' (12). Some find it hard to believe in an invisible God, but he has solved the problem in two ways:

❍ 'The only Son ... has shown us what God is like' (John 1:18). As we read the gospels, we are able to 'see' God, in Jesus.

❍ 'If we love each other, God lives in us ...'(12). This statement is astonishing — even outrageous, if we think about it. What John claims is that the unseen God who showed himself clearly in Jesus, is now showing himself today when Christians really love each other. Amazing!

If a neighbour or friend asked you 'What is God like?', how would you reply? If they came with you to your church, would they find it open to honest searchers? Pray that it will be.

DAY 86: WE CAN HAVE CONFIDENCE

Lord, open your word to my mind and heart, and open my heart and mind to your word.

1 John 4:13-21

Even in times of false teaching, doubt and confusion, 'we *can* know that we are living in him and he is living in us' (13, Jerusalem Bible).

How? 'God has given us his Spirit'. How can we know this? Partly, by the way the Spirit 'fills our hearts with his love' (Romans 5:5 — Reading 82). If I find I can love people unselfishly, this is contrary to my human nature. It must come from outside me, from the source of love (19). This gives me confidence that God has come into my life and made me his child (3:1). I need not fear meeting him (17)! Now John does not say that we *become* children of God by loving others, but that the love we find in our hearts for others, who also share our unloveliness, *shows* that the life of God is in us. Trees which look dead all winter, bud in Spring. The warmth of the sun brings life through the rising sap, but the visible evidence of that life is the fresh green leaves. If we claim to have the life but don't show the love, we are walking denials of God. This can provide others with concrete reasons for turning away from him (20,21).

If we lived in a dry place and discovered a well of clean water, we'd quickly share the news with those we loved. Just as naturally, John describes how he not only knows Jesus, but is 'telling others about him' (14). Love that does not include sharing the good news of Jesus is a poor kind of love.

DAY 87: NO OTHER WAY

'Let not thy word, O Lord, become a judgement upon us, that we hear it and do it not, that we know it and love it not, that we believe it and obey it not …' *(probably by St Thomas á Kempis)*

1 John 5:1-5

Can you remember moments that glowed with the reality of God?

❍ a time of worship when God was inexpressibly there, and you felt love all around you and within?

❍ a prayer, clearly and miraculously answered?

❍ a day when wonderful God-given gifts enabled you to meet great demands placed upon you?

Good. Treasure them. But in God's economy, a simple attitude or act of obedience reflects more clearly than any of these experiences (3), your love for him. The song writer, Don Francisco sings, 'Love is not a feeling, it's an act of the will.' Let's not get too sentimental about love. The best love is gutsy, earthy, costly — sometimes not even noticed. To love God has a lot more to do with *doing* what he says, than saintly looks or pious words.

Some people see the Christian journey only as a caricature, a chain-dragging obedience to a set of negative, boring, life-cramping rules. But 'his commands are not too hard for us' (3) when this is a response to his love for us, an expression of our love for him. It is the world (4,5) and the one ruling it (19) that sucks the joy out of life. Faith, love and obedience link us to the victory that denies this evil control over our lives.

Try to write a prayer which includes three words — love, trust, obey. Perhaps note it in your journal or the flyleaf of your Bible.

DAY 88: WITH ALL MY HEART

Think of one of the best things that ever happened to you. Why was it so good?

Psalm 103:1-12

'What God has done for us far exceeds anything we have done for or against him. The summary word for this excessive, undeserved, unexpected act of God is *salvation*... There is more to do than recognise the sheer fact of salvation and witness to it; there are unnumbered details of grace, of mercy, of blessing to be appreciated and savoured.' *(Eugene Peterson, 'Psalms, Prayers of the Heart')*

David relishes the telling of the things that God loves doing for his people (3-5) — forgiving, healing, rescuing, honouring, satisfying, renewing. Can you find some of them and mark them in your Bible? Which of these has given you the greatest blessing?

For all his praise, David is not just puffing up clouds of pious clichés: he knows God has rescued him from the uncertain future of 'the grave' (4, GNB) and beyond. He admits that what he has received from God is not what he deserves (10).

How great is God's love? *How* far away has he taken our sins (11,12)? However high we go, we can always go higher; however far East or West we go, we can always go further; however far we have come in our journey with God, there is always more love and grace to discover.

What does it mean for you to be saved? What dimensions of salvation would you like to explore further? Share these with God and ask him to help you.

DAY 89: LOVE IS FOR EVER

The words 'Poet, Philosopher, Failure' appear on a grave in England. Who wrote them, the dead man or his friends? The 1st century epitaph, 'I was not. I was. I am not. I care not.' says much the same thing: 'My life meant nothing.' Too many people feel like this. David directs his thoughts to the positive things God has done. Look for them in today's reading. Think of an epitaph that expresses the meaning and purpose that God wants to give to your life.

Psalm 103:13-22

David's song (13,14) assures us of God's protective tenderness for his children. The original Hebrew is linked with the word for womb. (The Mother-love of a Father-God? Sometimes we find that human metaphors for God are stretched to breaking point.)

We may feel our lives are no more significant than a wildflower's, a colourful dot in a waving crowd one day, dead the next (15-18). But the Lord's love is everlasting and we know, better than David knew, that we are everlasting too. God's love for us is reflected in our praise for him (20-22). Here, David, like the conductor of an orchestra, brings in heavenly hosts and earthly creatures one by one to praise God. Finally, he calls his soul to join them. (Remember Reading 87? We praise God by doing his will.)

Knowing God's love for us and singing his praise can give poise and purpose to our lives — but sometimes we don't feel up to this. There are places where we can share our experience of God's love and express our praise. It's hard trying to be a Christian on your own. Look for a good church, and join a small group there.

Light for the path

HAVE YOU SEEN THIS SIGN BEFORE? THE SCRIPTURE UNION LOGO IS A LAMP - A STYLISED VERSION OF THE CLAY LAMPS OF THE TIME OF JESUS.

This logo can be seen all around the world (see page 126). It was chosen to express the theme of Psalm 119 verse 105. 'Your word is a lamp to guide me'. Scripture Union wants to help people read the Bible. A torch or a street lamp helps us to see our way in the dark. So reading the Bible helps us to see the way to live in the world.

Foothold is one of Scripture Union's Bible resources. This introduces you to the whole range of Bible guides designed to suit people of all stages and ages.

But publishing Bible guides is not the only way Scripture Union workers try to open the Bible's message with people. Staff and trained volunteers can be found amongst school children, in holiday camps, sharing God's good news wherever kids gather in suburban centres and at holiday resorts. Scripture Union workers operate in partnership with local churches and community groups.

If you would like to find out more about Scripture Union's activities, programs and other resources contact your nearest Scripture Union office. The address is on page 126. Just mention *Foothold* when you write.

And keep watching this sign. You never know where you will see it next!

THE GOD WHO STAYS CLOSE

INTRODUCTION TO READINGS 90 TO 100, IN EXODUS, 2 CORINTHIANS AND JOHN.

'Where is God?' is a question so profound that only philosophers and children ask it. Is God the spirit within every living thing we see? Is God just a reflection of *me*, when I meditate most deeply? Is God the One who made the universe, then left it alone to run (or run down) itself?

The Bible gives us a different picture of God, directing us to the more helpful question, *'What is God like?'* The early biblical books reveal a God who is who he is, powerful, perfect, and personal, separate and different from what he has created.

But as we'll see in Exodus, God is not distant. Together with Moses and the Israelites, we shall wrestle with his character. God wants to come close to his people; sometimes they want to come close to him. God is holy, they are not.

God's relationship with his people has been described thus: 'In the Old Testament we see God *over* his people; in the gospels we see him *with* his people, and in the New Testament church *in* his people.' Though rigid, this is not a bad description of the way God has related to his people through the ages.

Paul, wrote to the Corinthians, battling against false teachers. They were trying to take people back to an understanding of God being *over* them. Paul insists that God's new covenant is a matter of the heart, God is *in* them.

We end in John's gospel, reading about those precious hours Jesus spent with his close friends giving them a crash course in true survival, just before he left them. 'Stay close', he said.

DAY 90: ENCOUNTER WITH GOD

'Come near to God, and he will come near to you.' (James 4:8) This God — what is he like? Write down two things about him that are real to you.

Exodus 19:1-19

Any teacher knows that if you try too early to show children that you actually *like* them, they may never learn to respect you. The children of Israel were still very young in their walk with God; they had recently (1) learned that he was very powerful, and that he was on their side. Now, before they encountered the nature-gods of Canaan, they had to learn that he was a great and holy God, not to be casually approached (10-12,16-19) Soon they would learn that unlike the nature gods (and unlike the contemporary gods of today's New-Age and other religions), he made precise moral demands of his people (see chapter 20).

Yet they had no need to feel alienated by his terrifying holiness as,

- provided they kept the covenant, they were treasured by God, specially chosen and precious (5).
- they had a mediator, a go-between (Moses).

This same God has chosen us and given us a new covenant and a better mediator (Hebrews 9:15).

The people of Israel prepared, both mentally and ritually (10-15) to meet with God. Rituals are outward, visible expressions of inner realities. They are often things we do habitually, without asking why — like singing 'Happy Birthday' and giving presents on family birthdays. It would be sad if those doing this for you didn't love you. Rituals are important, but only if they represent a truth. Think of what you do in church, or when preparing for church. Do they express truths about God that are real to you?

DAY 91: FACE TO FACE

'Prayer is a gift of God, and we shall never really pray unless continually we ask God for his gift of prayer. We need to experience prayer, like love, as a gift every day, a fresh gift, a gift far beyond what we deserve.' *(Mark Gibbard)*

Exodus 33:7-11

'They're all black belts in prayer, of course', said the mission representative casually, as he led us towards the prayer meeting in the mission retirement home. We shared briefly some of the things we had on our minds. Then, as we all prayed, the topics shared were one by one called up, as it were, interrogated, set upon and wrestled to the ground, with concentrated imagination, energy and authority. Images jostled in my mind as these frail octogenarians, like fearsome sumo wrestlers, stepped out into the world of spiritual reality, and walked and strove in it with confident mastery. Prayer like this had not been learned overnight, nor from a how-to-do-it manual.

So with Moses. It had been over forty years since his first back-pedalling encounter at the burning bush (Exodus 3) with 'I AM WHO I AM'. He hadn't fallen into this 'face to face' (11) relationship with God; he'd grown into it. The 'highs', the mountain top times with God, and the 'lows' of disappointment with himself and with others, had all been part of this growth. Since the last reading, no times had been higher nor lower. See, for example, chapters 20 and 32.

We learn to pray by praying. God provided the tent of meeting (7) for those who wanted to draw near to him. He is still available. Nothing lies outside the reach of prayer. Nothing, except what comes into God's 'no-go' area!

DAY 92: IF YOU WON'T, I CAN'T

Take time to reflect on all the ways in which you'd be in trouble without God in your life. Spell them out — it's too easy to just say 'everything'.

Exodus 33:12-23.

While Moses was up on the mountain with God, the people behaved in a way that was weak, stupid, and disobedient. Drastic steps then had to be taken to counteract the consequences of their actions (see chapter 32).

Here, God forgives them and promises that he will still take them on to the promised land (1,2). *But* — forgiveness is one thing, restoration is another. God refuses to go with them (3).

Moses is devastated and desperate. He pleads with God to reverse this decision (12-16). God agrees.

Have you met a Canaanite recently? Seen any Perizzites on TV? No? All the tribes mentioned in 34:11 have been 'dead meat' for two thousand years. The Israelites would have been too, but for one thing. Read verse 16 again. We, the church, are the spiritual inheritors of Israel. But by nature, Christians are no better than atheists or Zoroastrians. Nothing about us gives us the right to be — not our history, our buildings, our traditions, our music, our style — not even our doctrines. We exist only because of that Presence.

Pioneer missionary David Livingstone wrote in his diary: 'Lord, send me anywhere, only go with me.' Ask God to show you where to go with him this week. Don't bother much if you can't *feel* his presence (some do, some don't — usually I don't). Just remind him, and yourself, that he's promised to go with you (for example, Matthew 28:18-20), and that you need him. Desperately.

DAY 93: SHINING FACES

'Lift up your heart to God with humble love: and mean God himself, and not what you get out of him.'

(*The Cloud of Unknowing*, 14th C.)

Exodus 34:29-35

The Israelites' crass rebellion in the Golden Calf affair left them far from God. Yet, God in his grace restored his purposes for Israel and promised his presence with them (33:1,14). This chapter tells how God moves to again give Israel the covenant of the Law (34:1,2). Once more Moses is the mediator, the go-between. As he sets out to obey God, he is given a vision of God's greatness (34:6-8).

When Moses comes down from the mountain:

His face shines from his close encounter with God. Have you noticed the presence of God in other people? How does it show? Quiet joy? Purposeful love? Sheer goodness? Unselfconscious generosity?

He is unaware of it. Sometimes preachers tell us we should be radiant. We can pray for this, but if we try too hard to shine, this can lead to faking the joy or the love. Sooner or later the cracks in the mask will show up — disastrously. Better to seek God's presence and obey his word — and leave to him how others perceive us.

Some were afraid. The presence of God is an awesome thing. I have known Christians whose closeness to God has left me uncomfortable. But if we love God and continue to obey him, we need not fear.

Is there somebody who is, for you, an outshining of God's presence? Does she/he seem so close to God as to be beyond temptation, past need for prayer or encouragement? Don't believe it! Satan will have his claws into this person. Thank God for them and pray for them.

DAY 94: JESUS' LETTERS TO THE WORLD

Can you build a prayer from these quotes? 'I apologise for boasting, but once you know my qualities I can drop back into a quite brilliant humility.' *(Christopher Fry)*; 'The word itself comes from the Latin *humus*, which means fertile ground... But ... humility is one of those virtues that we can never attain by focusing on it.' *(Richard Foster)*

2 Corinthians 3:1-11

The church at Corinth, which Paul had planted, was in trouble. This was partly because some of its leaders were criticising Paul, and preaching a 'different gospel'. Paul writes to defend the true Gospel, and inevitably finds he is defending himself. This worries him, as it feels like boasting. Does he need to boast, he asks? Does he need letters, references, from important leaders in the church (as the false teachers evidently had)? No, Paul says, they, once immoral and unfaithful, the former thieves, drunkards, slanderers and cheats who now made up the Corinthian church (1 Corinthians 6:9-11) as renewed and reformed people, were 'our letter ...for everyone to read and understand ... written in our hearts by the Spirit of the living God' (2,3).

This leads Paul to thoughts about the agreement between God and his people, commonly called the Old Covenant, which we have been looking at in Exodus, and the new agreement (or New Covenant) brought existence through Jesus' death and resurrection. Work through the comparisons; Jeremiah 31:31-33 is helpful.

'Of one hundred people, one will read the Bible; the ninety nine will read the Christian.' *(D.L. Moody)* Thinking of this should not make us self-conscious, working hard at looking humble! But we can pray that people who meet us will be able to read Jesus' writing.

DAY 95: ONE THING I ASK

David, the warrior king, the man of strength and action, wrote: 'I ask only one thing, Lord: Let me live in your house every day of my life to see how wonderful you are and to pray in your temple' (Psalm 27:4).

Reflect on these times spent with God. How have they helped you find direction and stability for your life? What do you seek in meeting with God today?

2 Corinthians 3:12-18

How we imagine God affects how we live. So one of the aims of this book has been to help us learn more about God and his character. From that knowledge we can begin to imitate him, and grow more like him. The old fashioned word for this was 'godliness'. But to become like him,

- we must turn to the Lord (16), making a deliberate U-turn *away from* the things that blind us and come between us and Christ (GNB, 'veils'), and then *turn to* Christ, placing our loyalty and trust in him.
- we must 'fix our eyes' (4:18) on Christ. 'Show' (3:18) can be translated 'contemplate' or 'reflect', referring either to the process of giving Jesus our full attention, or the result. Either way, 'as the Spirit of the Lord works within us, we become more and more like him' (Living Bible).

Many experienced Christians say that they never *have* time for praying. They find they must *make* time for it. If you intend to continue making time with God and his word a regular habit, make arrangements now for something to help you in the same way. Scripture Union can help. See the inside back cover of this book for the next book or advice about other alternatives.

DAY 96: TOMORROW IS ANOTHER DAY

What do *you* worry about? What keeps you awake in the grey hours before dawn? Do you bring your worries to Jesus?

John 14:1-7

Imagine you're there. Use all your senses to recreate the feel of that upper room, the smell of the oil lamps, your emotions. Look back to chapter 13. Do you feel shame (3-6), confusion (21,22), discomfort (30) or terror (33,36)? Your world, which has centred on your great teacher and friend, is about to fall apart. You feel sick with fear. 'Don't be worried… I'm going there [ahead] to prepare a place for each of you' (1,2). Jesus is saying that there's room for everybody.

Your friend Thomas is worried: 'How can we know the way?' (There were no maps in those days.) Suddenly Jesus lifts the whole conversation by a couple of quantum leaps — 'I am the way.'

The Way We too have no map, for this life or the next, but we do have a Guide.
The Truth The universe can be a strange, mad, painful place, but Jesus is a great Anchor-point for our mind.
The Life If we're all created and cremated equal, what's the point? The point is that Jesus will be there for us at the end, so for now and later, there's a future and a hope.

Imagine losing, one by one, your home, your livelihood, your favourite possessions, your health, your special gifts, your partner. This can happen. What would then be left for you? Jesus remains always, waiting to lead you to the Father (6).

All of us have to walk the 'lonesome valley' at some point. Does the idea fill you with terror or joy?

DAY 97: EVEN GREATER THINGS

Surrounded by a world ignorant of God, hard, violent, arrogant, what effect can our prayers have? None, if God is not at work; enormous, if he is. Pray, pushing back the encircling darkness, making space for the living God.

John 14:8-14

To a Jew, God was infinite, almighty, and invisible. Poor Philip had problems grasping the idea (9) of God as finite, vulnerable and visible. 'Our God contracted to a span, incomprehensibly made man' *(Wesley)*. Jesus claimed (10) that his words were the words of God, his acts the acts of God. Someone has said that if Jesus wasn't God, he deserved an Oscar!

I hate turning wine into water, diluting the clear commands and promises of Scripture, saying, 'Of course it doesn't really mean what it says'. But what *does* verse 12 mean? What kind of world would it be if all Jesus' followers went around walking on water and raising the dead? Reading the context is always a good idea. We can see that by 'things', Jesus was referring to the miracles that show that he and the Father truly are one, that he is God (see John 2:11).

With the historical facts of the cross and the resurrection behind them, his disciples were able to make Jesus known to a greater degree than even he could at that time, and to a wider audience. The same is true for us.

The original promise (13) wasn't a blank cheque. 'In my name' (GNB) means 'as Jesus' representative', asking only for things in tune with the character and purposes of Jesus.

Think prayerfully over your next 24 hours — the expected encounters, the possibilities. Pray in Jesus' name, that he may be made real through your words and actions.

DAY 98: YOU ASK ME HOW I KNOW HE LIVES?

'This is the reason why we have no ease of heart and soul… we are seeking our rest in trivial things that cannot satisfy, and not seeking to know God, almighty, all-wise, all good. He is true rest.' *(Julian of Norwich).* Seek him.

John 14:15-31

The disciples are disturbed at the idea of Jesus going away. 'Don't worry', Jesus says, 'the world won't see me, but you will' (19). Judas says, 'How come?' Jesus explains that after he goes, as their love for him responds in obedience to his truth, he will become real to them through the Holy Spirit (16,17). The resurrection will become more than history, it will be living experience (19). Beware! Check out verses 15,21,23. Anything less than this love/obedience relationship with Jesus will leave you on the outside of the resurrection, looking in.

Counsellor, helper, advocate, comforter, Spirit —words to describe someone who advises, helps, encourages, defends, reassures or stimulates us to do what otherwise we could never do (16,17). The thrust of its meaning is that this Person would be, for the disciples and you, what Jesus was when he was with them.

How can it be, we ask, that Father, Son and Spirit are so One that if one comes to us, all come? (17,18,23) We should *try* to understand how God has revealed himself in Christ (7,9). This is given to us to experience and enjoy, not necessarily to understand fully.

When God comes to live within us, half a dozen other things will be true for us, Jesus says. Find these promises in today's reading. Choose one. Think about it as you pray. Reflect on it during the day.

DAY 99: STAY JOINED TO ME

The world around seems in great pain through poverty, violence, fear, lethargy, pride, materialism. We want to make a difference. I do too Lord. Start with me.

John 15:1-8

In Reading 64, on Psalm 80, we saw God's people Israel pictured as a vineyard planted by God. Now, says Jesus, there's a new vine — a new people of God — growing from him. Those who cut themselves off from him condemn themselves to emptiness — and judgement (6).

The branches of a grapevine have one purpose only — to produce grapes — you can't make furniture out of grape wood. Why are there Christians? To bear fruit. Read Galatians 5:22,23. Do you have ripe fruit in any of the nine areas described? Don't be discouraged if some fruit is green. With the life of Jesus flowing into you, and the light of God shining on you, spiritual photosynthesis will happen! Again, some of God's work on you will involve some pain (2), but pain with a loving purpose.

Grapes not only express the life of the vine, but bear the genes to reproduce it. Another way to be fruitful is to share your faith with others.

Our fruitfulness can 'make a difference'. God has taken the risk, and created a situation where his reputation hangs on the fruitfulness of Jesus' followers (8). Can you see openings for producing fruit?

'Stay joined to me and let my teachings become part of you' (7). For many, staying close to Jesus is a haphazard process, relying on a good feeling here, a happy turn of events there, a glimpse of God in nature, and so on. What intentional plans do you have for staying close to Jesus?

DAY 100: MORE THAN SERVANTS

A little book by Mrs H. Strahan, called *The Quiet Time*, was a very practical help to generations of students and others. On the last page, it warned not to miss the best thing of all: 'There is reward for the obedient disciple, there are power and authority for the faithful disciple, there is glory of achievement for the zealous disciple; but there is the joy of His presence, and the shining of His face, for those who love Him for Himself alone.'

John 15:9-17

According to the American constitution, the pursuit of happiness is a fundamental right. But millions have sadly discovered that pursuing it is not the best way to find happiness. Jesus gives us some better things to set our hearts on.

Obedience (10) — the only way to keep on experiencing his love.
Service (13) — Jesus laid down his life, not only in his dying but in his living; in a small way, we can walk in his shoes (12).
Going out (16) — showing (to 'produce fruit') and telling the world what a good God we have.
Loving each other (12,17) — sacrificial practical love between people whose love is centred on and nourished by Jesus.

To those who choose to respond to his choice (16), Jesus promises not happiness, though this may well come, but joy (deep-down satisfaction + delight) — not just any old joy, but *his* joy (11; also 14:27).

'The main thing', a friend of mine says, 'is that the main thing remain the main thing.' What is the main thing in your life? What plans do you have for making sure that it stays at the centre of your vision? Give them to God.

WHERE TO FIND

Scripture Union

AUSTRALIA:
PO Box 2915, Fitzroy DC, Victoria 3065

CANADA:
1885 Clements Road, Unit 226, Pickering, Ontario L1W 3V4

FIJI:
PO Box 1278, Suva

HONG KONG:
St Andrew's Centre, 138 Nathan Road, Kowloon

MALAYSIA:
386 Jalan 5/59, 46000 Petaling Jaya, Selangor

NEW ZEALAND:
PO Box 760, Wellington

PAKISTAN:
8/4 Modern Colony, Kot-Lakhpat, Lahore 54770

PAPUA NEW GUINEA:
PO Box 280, University, NCD

SINGAPORE:
#03-07, 7 Armenian Street, Singapore 179932

SOUTH AFRICA:
PO Box 291, Rondebosch 7700, Cape Town

UK:
207-209 Queensway, Bletchley, Milton Keynes, Bucks. MK2 3EB, England

USA:
Suite 215, 150 Strafford Avenue, Wayne, PA 19087

INTERNATIONAL OFFICE:
59 Princess Road West, Leicester LE1 6TR, England